Contents

Group Lesson Plans

[handwritten note: See folder from Susan allis in black file on "Friendship" Groups]

GROUP COUNSELING

For School Counselors:
A Practical Guide

By Greg Brigman
and Barbara Earley

J. Weston Walch, Publisher
Portland, Maine

Users' Guide
to
Walch Reproducible Books

As part of our general effort to provide educational materials which are as practical and economical as possible, we have designated this publication a "reproducible book." The designation means that purchase of the book includes purchase of the right to limited reproduction of all pages on which this symbol appears:

Here is the basic Walch policy: We grant to individual purchasers of this book the right to make sufficient copies of reproducible pages for use by all students of a single teacher. This permission is limited to a single teacher, and does not apply to entire schools or school systems, so institutions purchasing the book should pass the permission on to a single teacher. Copying of the book or its parts for resale is prohibited.

Any questions regarding this policy or requests to purchase further reproduction rights should be addressed to:

Permissions Editor
J. Weston Walch, Publisher
P.O. Box 658
Portland, ME 04104-0658

—*J. Weston Walch, Publisher*

Cover photograph taken by CLEO Photography

3   4   5   6   7   8   9   10

01–2550

ISBN 0-8251-1785-2

About the Authors

Barbara Earley, NCC, Ed.S., is a middle school counselor in Lawrenceville, Georgia. Greg Brigman, Ph.D., is an assistant professor of counseling at Clemson University. In 1986 the two authors were named National Middle School Counselors of the Year by the American School Counselors Association. In 1987 *The Complete Book of Peer Helping*, which they authored, won a national award from the ASCA.

The authors:

- Train and supervise school counseling students
- Teach a Group Counseling for School Counselors course
- Train and supervise teachers to be school counselors in the Elementary Counselor Institute at Georgia State University.
- Teach a group-counseling course for school counselors at Georgia State University.
- Conduct workshops for counselors in the areas of organizing and administering a coordinated developmental school-counseling program, peer helping, and group counseling.
- Teach staff-development courses for teachers, focusing on classroom management and motivation.
- Lead parent/teen communication seminars and were part of a team that wrote the materials used in a drug abuse prevention program which was awarded a national grant.
- Design curriculum in the areas of study skills, peer helping, career education, and school counseling.
- Coordinate with administrators in devising and implementing plans for community and school improvement.

Other counseling materials by the authors:

- *Peer Helping: A Training Manual.* J. Weston Walch, Publisher, Portland, ME, 1990.
- *Student Success Training,* a cassette tape on motivation, study skills, relaxation, and imagery. Ocean Publishers, Clemson, SC, 1987.

Contributing Authors

The following contributors are counselors in the Gwinnett County School System, Lawrenceville, Georgia.

Elementary Counselors

- Gwendolyn Baity Cheatham
- Annette Hildreth
- Sherry Stahler
- Pat Crate (Fulton County Schools)

Middle School Counselors

- John Patrick Huerta
- Sharon Pitman
- Marge Snider

High School Counselors

- Maryanne Brannigan Grimes
- Gayl Kelley

Consultant

- Mary Joe Hannaford

Introduction

Group Counseling for School Counselors is a practical guide for leading counseling groups for school-aged children and youth. We developed the structured session plans because we had a need for them as school counselors and because similar material was not available.

This book contains three essentials for counselors working with youth in groups:

1. a description of group-leadership skills and the group-counseling process;

2. detailed session outlines;

3. a range of group topics that cover the most important themes in working with young people.

This book will be useful to you if:

- You have just received your degree in school counseling and you would like some practical materials for implementing groups.

- You are already a counselor, but you sense a lack of support for your group program from teachers and administrators.

- You are overwhelmed. You are one person, and you cannot possibly meet the needs of everyone. Sometimes you are under so much stress that you are not able to give 100% of yourself to the job.

- You have been a counselor for many years, but the job description has changed. You have always done permanent records, schedules, testing, and college preparation, and now are supposed to lead groups and teach parent courses.

- You feel good about your counseling program and you think you are a competent counselor, but lately you have started to ask, "Is this all there is?"

Our Philosophy of School Counseling

Our focus is on meeting the developmental needs of students through the use of classroom guidance, small groups, and individual counseling with students. This book provides ideas for using groups with students, and also for teachers and parents.

In our school we emphasize that groups are for everyone. We want teachers, parents, and students to see our program as a preventive, developmental program. Everyone can benefit from learning conflict resolution, communication and friendship skills, and building/maintaining high self-esteem. We want to remove or lessen any stigma attached to being in a counseling group. We see counselors as partners with teachers, administrators, and parents in the process of education.

Four main themes run through our counseling program:

1. Teaching students to take responsibility for their actions.
2. The concept of mutual respect—respect for self and others.
3. Training in basic life-management skills: communication, decision making, problem solving, and conflict resolution.
4. The belief that students who feel good about themselves and have positive relationships with others achieve more and are more successful in and out of school.

We believe that counselors should be leaders in encouraging a positive school climate; mental health and developmental psychology specialists who make a positive difference in the lives of students; program managers; educators who maximize the potential of students; and advocates of children.

We also believe that school counselors should have a core theory which helps them explain human behavior to students, parents, teachers, and administrators. There are many theories from which to choose. The choice of theory does not seem to greatly change the effectiveness of the counselor. It is very helpful to have a systematic plan or rationale for using various techniques. Corey's *The Theory and Practice of Group Counseling* (1985) gives an overview for integrating various techniques from different theories at specific stages of the group's development. An understanding of theory and knowledge of techniques for leading groups are goals we urge for all school counselors.

The core theory upon which our program is built is Adlerian. Some of the key Adlerian principles that guide our work are:

- A holistic view of man rather than an atomistic view.
- A respect for self and others as social equals who all have intrinsic value.
- An education model which assumes normality, versus a medical model that assumes illness.

- Problems are social in nature and born out of lack of information rather than illness.

- The importance of seeing the world through the other person's eyes in order to help redirect one toward more effective and cooperative living.

- People are goal-directed and growth-oriented.

- All behavior has the goal or purpose of achieving significance, security, or belonging.

- Facilitating the development of skills essential for effective living and learning is a main role of the counselor.

Other theories that blend well with Alder's, and from which we borrow techniques, include: Person-Centered (Rogers, Carkhuff); Cognitive (Ellis, Beck, Burns); Behavioral/Multimodal (Lazarus, Keats); and Reality Therapy (Glasser).

Regardless of your theoretical inclination, there are some attitudes and beliefs which are essential to effective helping. Rogers et al. (1967) and Truax and Carkhuff (1967) found empathy, unconditional regard, congruence, nonpossessive warmth, and genuineness to be the key attitudes. In addition, Combs et al. (1969) determined that effective counselors share certain beliefs and perceptions, which include:

1. People are worthy of respect and are capable of solving their own problems.

2. Behavior is predictable and understandable, and it is a product of unfolding from within, rather than molding by external events.

3. Effective counselors perceive themselves as fundamentally adequate, dependable, and likeable; and their role is one of freeing rather than controlling.

4. Effective counselors perceive themselves as being concerned with people rather than things, and they approach others pragmatically.

Because of our theoretical base and core beliefs, and because of our experience leading groups with children in schools (grades 5–12) and with adults, our style is directive. Our goal is to teach skills and increase awareness in order to help participants become more effective in their relationships, their learning, and their work. It is important to have group members working toward clear goals. Some support for this view comes from Prout and DeMartino (1986), who conducted a meta-analysis of school-based studies of psychotherapy. Group and behavioral theory interventions that targeted observed behaviors and problem-solving abilities were found to be more effective than other approaches. Structured groups offer increased accountability to both the leader and the participants since the goals of the leader and the participants are explicit and congruent (Day and Sharacio, 1980).

The group plans in this book are for the most part structured and goal-directed. The counselor has an agenda and is active and facilitative. This approach to group counseling in schools appears to be the predominant one in the United States. We believe that counselors are creative and innovative and can use structured activities as springboards or vehicles to reach counseling goals.

We do not expect counselors using these plans to slavishly follow every point, but rather to pick and choose the material that best fits their unique situations. Trotzer (1977) made some specific suggestions about using structured activities that apply: 1) the counselor should thoroughly know the exercise and feel secure using it; and 2) the counselor should be fully aware of the intent of the exercise, its process, and the kinds of outcomes that can be expected.

Why Group Counseling?

Dinkmeyer (1969) provided a solid rationale for group counseling. He emphasized that since children are social beings whose growth and development take place in groups, it seems logical that they would be comfortable meeting and discussing issues with their peers. Within this setting the counselor can observe the kinds of social relationships the children share with each other and learn more about these interactions than he or she could in individual counseling.

The following are some additional reasons for group counseling in the schools:

1. Group counseling is considered a primary role of the school counselor by the American School Counselor Association.

2. In a March 1988 article in the *School Counselor* by Wilgus and Shelley regarding the role of the elementary-school counselor, teachers ranked individual and group counseling as the top two actual and ideal counselor functions.

3. In a national survey of school counselors by Bowman, which appeared in the March 1987 *School Counselor*, counselors at all levels agreed that small-group counseling is vital and practical.

4. Group counseling is more efficient than one-to-one counseling and often is more appropriate. Many student concerns involve poor peer relations, under-achievement, and low self-esteem. The support students can receive in a group setting is often more powerful than one-to-one support from a counselor. Whether the problem is friendship, divorce, loss, or some other concern, it is one thing for a student to be reassured by an adult (the counselor) that he or she is not alone, but quite another matter to hear and see that same support in the safe environment of a group led by a skilled counselor.

5. Group counseling expands your services. If you are a first-year counselor, consider conducting groups as a top priority. There are students who need more than the limited one-to-one time available from you. Conducting groups allows you to offer systematic counseling to more students.

6. In a group setting there are more insights, ideas, confirming messages, and information shared than any one individual could give.

7. Students get a chance to know the counselor during the group meetings and are then more likely to come in for individual counseling if there is a need. Conversely, a student who sees the counselor in individual sessions may be more willing to join a group. By observing individuals participating in group activities, the counselor is in a better position to determine if additional counseling or referral is needed.

8. Students live in a social world. The group represents a microcosm of their world in which they can practice new behavior that is more adaptive and constructive.

9. Group counseling can be preventive, because it stresses the life-management skills needed to deal with problems before they become crises.

10. The idea of the group offering a supportive environment should not be underestimated. Not only is anxiety reduced when students learn that they are not alone with their concerns, but a sense of belonging and support can replace feelings of loneliness, isolation, and helplessness.

There are many compelling reasons for offering group counseling in the schools. The purpose of this book is to assist school counselors in offering group support.

Group Counseling: An Overview

Types of Groups

Counselors often find themselves dealing individually with several students who have very similar concerns. These concerns may be developmental or crisis-oriented. Group counseling allows the counselor to focus on the students' needs while providing an opportunity for positive interactions and peer support.

Group counseling in the school setting can be divided into two categories: developmental/preventive groups, and special-concerns groups. The developmental groups include topics that address normal developmental skills and tasks (Thornburg, 1974; Maslow, 1968; Havighurst, 1953), e.g., friendship skills, decision-making skills, communication skills, and self-esteem. Although these topics are often introduced through classroom guidance, students referred for a developmental group address these topics in greater depth. Typical reasons for referral are: behavior problems, poor peer relations, underachievement, and low self-esteem. These topics can be effectively addressed in a group by focusing on interpersonal skills, self-esteem, and decision making/problem solving. Extensive educational research in the last twenty years clarifies the importance of effective social skills and high self-esteem to academic success (Hops & Cobb, 1974; Cartledge & Milburn, 1978; Wooster & Carson, 1982). Group counseling is an effective tool for the counselor who wants to help students improve in both of these critical areas.

The other category for group counseling is special concerns: topics such as divorce, loss, pregnancy, or a recent move. These groups are for students who have some special problem or concern that differentiates them from their classmates.

Logistics of Group Counseling

School counseling groups meet 6–10 times, with each meeting lasting 30–60 minutes, depending on the age of the students. The meetings occur during the school day, and teacher approval is obtained.

Group size is determined by the age of the students and purpose of the group. Generally, the younger the students, the smaller the group. Most groups include 5–10 students. One or more "role models" (model students who are respected by their peers) are included in most groups. According to Myrick (1987), "experienced school counselors prefer to work with 5–6 and no more than 7–8. Having fewer members allows more participation by each person in the group."

Through an information letter, parents can be made aware of student participation in a group. We recommend a form letter signed by the parent giving permission for participation. Sample letters are included in each lesson plan.

The younger the student, the shorter each meeting. The chart below shows typical times for different grade levels:

Grade Level	*Average Length of Each Meeting*
K–3	20–30 minutes
4–5	30–40 minutes
6–12	45–60 minutes (one class period)

Once you have developed a system for providing group counseling, it is important that you maintain its structure. Canceling or postponing sessions will impair the integrity of the program. If group counseling is to become one of the educational objectives of your school, students, teachers, parents, and administrators must understand what it is and know what to expect from it.

Gaining Support from Teachers, Administrators, and Parents

A group-counseling program cannot work within a school system without the support of teachers, administrators, and parents. To gain their support you must identify and clarify common goals. Once common goals are established, you must make a case for group counseling as a means to attain those goals.

Teachers want their students to participate in a counseling group once they understand what a counseling group is. What you say at the PTA, in newsletters, at faculty meetings, and in conferences should clearly describe the purpose and expected outcomes of group counseling; explanations should always be couched in terms of common goals.

For teachers, academic success and appropriate behavior are the most appealing of these common goals. Never assume that telling teachers once is enough. Provide teachers with handouts that describe the goals and objectives of group counseling. Explain your program to individual teachers who meet with you about specific children. Soon your teachers will be referring students to groups and describing groups to parents during conferences. When teachers are able to explain counseling groups to parents, you have gained their support.

Similar strategies work for gaining the support of administrators. Administrators try to juggle limited resources for the greatest good. Group counseling helps not only students, but parents and teachers as well. It is a means for systematically reaching the students who normally capture most of the administrators' time: children with behavior problems, academic problems, or attendance problems. When group counseling is presented as a way to reach these students, administrators will take notice, especially if you make your case before the start of the school year, when administrators are less harried and more able to listen.

When a child has a problem with grades, relationships, or family, the parents have a problem, too. A parent is more likely to support his or her child's involvement in a group if you make a direct connection between the child's problem and the topics addressed in groups: effective communication, self-esteem, stress management, goal-setting, and so forth. You should make it clear to parents that group counseling is not group therapy. Group counseling is not based on a medical model; it is based on an educational model which assumes normality, not illness. The group sessions are part of an educational curriculum based on sound, widely accepted principles.

Group counseling is not a familiar topic to most people, including educators. The more that teachers, administrators, and parents understand, the more they will support you.

Getting Started

By gaining the support of teachers, administrators, and parents, you have built a solid base for your group-counseling program. Next you need to do the following:

1. Explain the group offerings to the students during the first two or three weeks of class when you are informing them of the different counseling services available. Leave sign-up forms in each class and have a box or basket at your office door where students can pick up or turn in their forms.

2. Develop or review lesson plans for groups you will offer. Don't try to "wing it." The groups offered should meet the needs of your school. The lesson plans in this book were developed over a number of years based on: 1) needs assessments from teachers, students, parents, and administrators; 2) developmental theory; 3) counseling research; and 4) accepted practices endorsed by the American Association of School Counselors.

3. Around the end of September, send a referral sheet out to teachers. Also let parents know about the groups through PTA presentations and newsletters.

4. By the time you get teacher referral forms and student and parent requests back, you will probably realize you have more students than you can handle. Keep a list of students who are not included in the first round of groups. Send them a note explaining that the group is filled and they will be placed on a list for the next group.

5. Conduct pre-group interviews or screening. (See next section.)

6. Send invitations on the morning of the first meeting.

By following these six recommendations, you will ensure the success of your group-counseling program.

Before the First Meeting: Pre-Group Screening

There are several reasons to meet individually with students who have been recommended by teachers and parents for group counseling:

1. To determine the appropriateness of the particular group for this student. It is your decision to determine who will be in the group. Certain students might be detrimental to the progress of the group. When teachers ask why Billy isn't in your group, you can say, "It is not appropriate for him to be in this group. I am seeing him individually and I am working with his parents."

2. To give information about the nature of the group and your expectations regarding attendance, confidentiality, and so forth.

3. To gain commitment from the student regarding attendance, participation, and confidentiality. (Participation should be voluntary. If the student decides not to participate, advise the referring parent or teacher that when or if the student decides to voluntarily join the group, this service will be available—as soon as the next group begins.)

4. To help the student identify a goal(s) to work on in the group.

5. To clarify the student's expectations about the nature of the group.

6. To comply with ethical standards of the counseling profession (AACD, ASCA, AGSW).

This screening meeting usually takes approximately 10–15 minutes. Set aside a two-hour block per group for these interviews. What you gain is student understanding and commitment and parent awareness and permission. If the student agrees to participate, the student is asked to take a group information or consent form home.

Here is an outline for a screening meeting:

Pre-Group Interview Outline

1. Introduction
   a. General description of group (number of meetings, topics and so forth)
   b. Why the student is being asked to participate
   c. Participation is voluntary

2. What can be gained
   a. Meet new people
   b. Work on goals
   c. Learn new skills

3. Goal(s)

    a. Help student select a general goal (goal more defined during group meetings)

    b. Goals may change and are the business of the student

4. Expectations

    a. Attendance, participation, and confidentiality

    b. Check student expectations

5. Explain the Parent and Teacher forms and when to return them to the counselor

6. Brief summary and emphasis on positive aspects of group

The screening process allows you to be in a better position to decide who is appropriate for the kind of groups you are offering. No one else can make this decision as skillfully as you. You know best your skills, the nature of the children participating, the content of the group, and the readiness of each individual screened.

Helpful Hints for Leading Groups

The following guidelines will help your first group meetings run smoothly, thus ensuring the success of future sessions.

1. Have 2–3 role models in each group, unless the group is for a special concern such as divorce or loss. Modeling is a powerful learning tool that may explain why positive change frequently occurs more rapidly in a group setting. In general, we prefer heterogeneous grouping. In each group we have problem students, "normal" students, and role models. We generally would not recommend a group composed only of children with behavior problems, since they would not have appropriate role models. Glavin (1980), in his research on cooperative learning, supported mixed-ability grouping.

2. Group process is often more important than group content. It is important to help the members become aware of how they interact with one another, and the different roles they play in the group. Helping them connect how they operate in the group with how they behave in general is part of the process of counseling.

3. It is the interaction of the group members and what they learn from each other that becomes most important. Your lesson plan is only a vehicle for this learning. When an important issue emerges from the lesson plan, it is often more productive to explore this issue than to complete the lesson plan.

4. You need carefully planned topics and sequence. Don't come to the group without a plan. Remember: this experience is an educational counseling group, not a therapy group.

5. A group size of 5–10 works best. A group that is too small lacks diverse views and styles; it also makes having role models more difficult. More than 10 means less talk time per member and makes it harder to build trust and support. In general we recommend fewer students per group for younger children and for special-concern groups.

6. Six to ten sessions are typical. This number allows enough time to accomplish some goals. It's also short enough to create a sense of urgency. Some special-concern groups may require more than ten sessions to accomplish goals.

7. Provide each teacher with a group schedule and list of students in each group. A permission form from the teacher whose class the student will miss is suggested (see Forms section). Keeping teachers informed is good public relations.

8. Make group participation voluntary. You have a greater chance of reaching the goals of the group if participants have a choice.

9. To inform parents of their child's participation in a group, you may wish to send home an informational letter. This letter can also be a public-relations tool.

Groups of special concern, such as divorce or death, may need parent permission. You and your administrator may wish to decide how information is to be handled. Elementary-school counselors typically get permission for group counseling. Middle-school counselors may just send letters home to the parents. High-school counselors may not even inform parents or make them aware of participation.

10. Be consistent regarding the day of week, the time, and the place of meetings.

11. Have students complete an anonymous evaluation at the end of the group (see Sample Forms section). The evaluation provides the leader with helpful information for future planning.

12. Give general feedback to faculty and parents about the progress of groups based on evaluations. (E.g., 40 students participated in groups this quarter. 90% rated the experience as helpful or very helpful and would recommend that a friend participate.) Providing evaluative information helps develop support for your counseling program.

13. If you are just beginning, do not start with too many groups. It is better to have success with one group, then build slowly. We recommend that you start with developmental groups before beginning special-concerns groups. As your skills increase, you are better able to handle issues that have more emotional depth.

14. Tape some of your group sessions. Schedule the hour after the group meets to listen to the tape. You cannot improve if you don't listen to what you're doing. If you have video equipment, you may want to tape a key session, because evaluating your body language is very important. (Of course, you need to follow ethical guidelines regarding taping audio or video. See ASCA Ethical Guidelines in the Ethics section.)

15. A typical group session may be broken down this way:

    5–10 minutes: Icebreaker

    5 minutes: Review of last session (by participants)

    5–10 minutes: Reporting on goal or assignment progress by participants (if appropriate to group)

    20–25 minutes: Skill/awareness-building activity and discussion

    5–10 minutes: Wrapping up and summarizing, ending with participants completing one of the following open-ended sentences:

    > In today's meeting:
    >   I learned . . . .
    >   I relearned . . . .
    >   I was surprised that . . . .
    >   I was pleased that . . . .

16. It is important to model how you want your group to respond. If you want enthusiastic and attentive participation, then you need to act that way yourself. Give the group all of you, even though new students are waiting to register and you have an appointment the next hour with a student contemplating suicide.

This group may be the only affective training and group experience these students will get in twelve years of school.

Now you are ready to begin, and you have programmed success into your plan. You have developed support for your group-counseling program and are beginning with a group or groups you feel capable of leading successfully. You have a clear plan for each group session and the skills to facilitate the group process. You have set a workable number of group sessions with appropriate time limits and number of participants. You have screened group members and feel comfortable that they are appropriate for the group. Now you can enjoy the experience of skillfully providing a worthwhile service for your school.

What to Expect at Different Stages of the Group

It is helpful to be aware of the stages of group development as you prepare to lead your groups. We offer the following summary of three group stages to help you in your planning.

■ Stage 1: Trust–Orientation

In this stage, students get to know each other, establish trust, and decide how they fit into the group and how involved they will be. It usually takes three sessions for students to learn each other's names and to feel comfortable about being in the group. The leader provides more structured activities at this stage, and helps students identify goals.

■ Stage 2: Work–Productivity

The working stage is when the most insights and behavior changes occur. In an 8-session group, sessions 4–6 will contain most of the "work" of the group. This is the time when goals are acted on outside of the group, and experimenting with behavior occurs inside the group. If the necessary conditions of trust, empathy, and hope have developed, students will gain from feedback, confrontation, and increased self-awareness and self-disclosure.

■ Stage 3: Closure–Consolidation

The consolidation stage begins by session 7 of an 8-session group. There is usually a feeling of community—sharing and caring—if sessions 1–6 have been successful. The need to summarize, solidify changes, carry learning over to the world outside the group, and attain closure characterizes this stage. Session 8 might elicit responses like "I wish it wasn't over" and "Can we do this again?" It seems that just when you get a group going in the right direction, it's time to stop. You may decide to continue the group for a finite period, or you may be content to know that cohesiveness, cooperation, and learning have taken place. The benefits for some students will be wonderfully evident, and for others you will never know.

Here are some process questions for the different stages of group development.

■ Stage 1: Trust–Orientation

- What do you want to achieve by participating in this group?
- What are some concerns, doubts, and fears you have about being in this group?
- What would you most like to say you have learned at the end of this group?
- What do you need to give in order to get what you want from this group?
- What rules do we need to work out together, in order to feel safe and enjoy ourselves?

■ *Stage 2: Work–Productivity*

- How did you feel during this activity?
- What did you learn from this experience?
- How can you apply what you have learned today?
- What can you do this week to practice what you have learned?

■ *Stage 3: Closure–Consolidation*

- What are some of the most important things you have learned about yourself?
- How can you continue to practice what you have learned?
- What is one way you have changed during this group?
- What has been the most helpful part of this group for you?
- What is a goal you have set for yourself?
- How do you feel about the group ending?

Another way to look at the stages of group development is to consider two different functions of all groups: The task function, which is mostly cognitive, concerned with specific tasks and the exchange of information and ideas; and the maintenance function, which is concerned with feelings, attitudes, and the way group members relate to each other (Luft, 1984).

The four task-related issues of a group are:

1. Orientation: Who is here and what is going to happen? (Stage 1)
2. Norm Development: What are the rules regarding behavior, participation, and disagreement? (Stage 1)
3. Productivity: Getting things done and solving problems. (Stage 2)
4. Closure: Ending the group and applying what has been learned. (Stage 3)

The four maintenance-related issues of a group are:

1. Inclusion: Do I fit, belong? Can I trust the group? (Stage 1)
2. Control: Do I have influence, choice, and power? (Stage 1)
3. Affection: Do I feel close to the group? Is the climate warm? (Stage 2)
4. Closure: Ending the group and letting go. (Stage 3)

Shutz (1958) concluded that the first three maintenance issues are essential in order for any group to function productively. Members must feel that they are included, that they have some control, and that they are appreciated in order for the group to move to the productive stage of group work.

It is important for group leaders to facilitate the group's movement through these stages. If you begin to have problems at one stage, it is an indication that there are unresolved issues at the previous stage. (For example, not solving problems effectively may indicate a need to spend more time on norm development—how to disagree and solve conflict.)

As illustrated above, Stage 1 of our model of group development corresponds to the first two task and maintenance issues. Stage 2 corresponds to the third task and maintenance issues and Stage 3 corresponds to the fourth issues of task and maintenance.

It is beyond the scope of this book to deal with the stages of group development in more detail. For further reading, *Theory and Practice of Group Counseling* by Gerald Corey (1985) gives an excellent description of group stages. For specific techniques counselors can use to facilitate learning and growth at each stage, see *Group Techniques* by Gerald Corey et al. (1986).

Group Leadership Skills:
Keys to Success

One of the most important ingredients for successful group counseling is the skill of the group leader. Take time to honestly evaluate your skill level, experience, and course-work background. There is no substitute for supervised practice. Developing your skills is an ongoing process. Jim Gumaer, in an article in *The School Counselor* (1986), stated that "at a minimum level, graduating counselors should have passed successfully a group theory course, a group counseling practicum, and a supervised internship involving several counseling groups. . . . " If you do not have this background, we highly recommend that you obtain it. In addition, it is very helpful to co-lead groups. If you are the only counselor in your school, try co-leading a group with another counselor or therapist in your area. Taping your group sessions and having a qualified counselor give you feedback is also very beneficial.

The group-leadership skills that follow are basic and very effective. Simply reading them will not help. Listening to a tape of your group session and identifying which skills you used or did not use can be a powerful way to recognize your strengths and weaknesses.

■ *Seven Group Leadership Skills*

Personalizing
Structuring
Modeling
Connecting
Responding to each comment
Involving everyone
Summarizing

Personalizing: There are two important parts to this skill. The first is making sure the group is sitting in a circle so everyone can see everyone else's face without having to move. The second is making sure you know the names of all group members and use their names frequently when responding to their comments.

Structuring: This skill is used to explain the topic and time limit. Structuring is also used to get the discussion back on the topic when it digresses. *Example:* "For the next few minutes we'll be discussing friendship." When Maria starts getting off the topic, you might say, "I'd like to hear about that, Maria, but I'm concerned that we won't finish if we don't move on."

Modeling: Showing the group how you want them to respond. The leader usually goes first when everyone is asked to respond. *Example:* "Is everyone ready? Good, I'll go first . . . . "

Connecting: Building a sense of belonging and acceptance by helping the participants to see that others share their ideas and concerns. *Example:* "Who else has had that experience?" "How many of you have ever felt that way?" Another way to connect is to link the comments of the participants. "Juan, that sounds a lot like what Venetta was saying earlier." "Carl, I've noticed that you and Jim enjoy doing a lot of the same things. Can anyone else remember an idea some of us had in common?"

Responding to Each Comment: To encourage participants to discuss freely, it is important to reinforce each comment. Using their names is important. Examples: "OK, Maria, thank you. Lucy, how about you?" The leader can paraphrase the participant's comment: "So, Carl, you like to be with people who share some of your interests." Reflecting feelings is also a reinforcing response that shows you understand. "Jenny, you seem to feel pretty excited about that." This skill is especially important at the beginning of a group. It sets the tone. Making it safe to respond is critical.

Involving Everyone: Two techniques to get everyone involved are the go-round and the hand-raise. The go-round lets everyone know you expect a response from each group member. When using the go-round, give some time before beginning. The leader usually goes first. "I'd like you to think of some qualities you look for in a friend. I'll give you a moment to think of two or three, then we will go around and hear the ideas from each of you." Or: "For the next few minutes I'd like us to think of things you enjoy doing for fun. I will give you a minute to think of three or four things, then we will go around the circle and hear from everyone." If a group member does not have a response when the time comes, ask; "Would you like me to come back to you?" or "I'll check back with you in a minute." In addition, good eye contact and looking interested in each comment, nodding your head, and asking follow-up questions are important ways to keep participants involved. The hand-raise technique simply involves asking participants to raise their hands if the statement applies. Often the request to raise your hand is done non-verbally when the leader models raising a hand. "How many of you have ever been in a group where one person tried to dominate?" (leader raises a hand).

In addition to the go-round and some "How many of you" hand-raise questions, use the non-verbal behaviors of eye contact, leaning forward, and looking interested. It also helps to ask clarifying questions.

Summarizing: This skill can be used during the discussion or at the end. The leader can summarize or ask participants to summarize. The summary brings the focus back to the purpose of the discussion. An open-ended and personalized summary is often effective. *Example:* "We are almost out of time, and I would like for us to think about what we have talked about. What are some of the things we discussed?" The leader fills in any gaps. "To end, I would like you to complete this sentence: 'One thing I learned or relearned today was . . . . ' I'll give you a minute to think, then we will hear from everyone."

In order for these skills to be effective, the group leader must communicate certain attitudes such as:

     acceptance
     being non-judgmental
     warmth
     friendliness
     enthusiasm
     avoiding sarcasm

Some non-verbal behaviors that go with these attitudes are:

     good eye contact
     leaning forward
     looking interested

These group-leadership skills, attitudes, and non-verbal behaviors are basic to effective group leadership. For a more detailed explanation of skills for leading groups, see Corey (1985).

Ethics

As professional counselors, we must be aware of and comply with the ethical guidelines of AACD, ASCA, and ASGW. Since the ASGW guidelines are specific to group counseling, a copy of the 18 guidelines is presented below. The newly revised ASGW ethical guidelines will become available as this book is in press. You may obtain a copy of the new guidelines by writing AACD at 5497 Stevenson Ave., Alexandria, Virginia 22304 or calling (703) 823-9800.

Ethics are not black-and-white issues. If you have questions regarding some practices, we encourage you to consult with a colleague, pinpoint the ethical issue, and discuss the alternatives and possible consequences. If you are still in doubt, your state licensing board (if you are in a state that licenses counselors) has an ethics committee. ASGW and AACD also have ethics committees. Any of these three groups would be willing to discuss the issue with you.

Two journal articles that address the topic of ethical guidelines for group counseling are:

1. "Ethical Issues and Group Work with Children" by Cynthia Terres and Marva Larrabel in the February 1985 *Elementary School Guidance and Counseling Journal*. The authors apply the ethical guidelines for group leaders (adopted by the Association of Specialists in Social Work) to working with children in elementary and middle school. Some key points include: requirements for pre-group interviews, continuous attention to confidentiality, and counselor competence.

2. "Working with Groups: Training Group Leaders in Ethical Decision Making" by Jim Gumaer and Larry Scott in the November 1985 *Journal for Specialists in Group Work*. The authors describe a method for training group leaders in ethical decision making, using ASGW's ethical guidelines, case vignettes, and Carkhuff's three goals of helping. Vignettes covering all 18 points of ASGW's ethical guidelines for group leaders are presented with a survey of 122 ASGW members' responses to the same case situations.

By taking the time to understand the ethical issues involved in group counseling, you will be in a better position to protect the legal and ethical rights of your students and yourself.

Ethical Guidelines for Group Leaders[1]

■ *Preamble*

One characteristic of any professional group is the possession of a body of knowledge and skills and mutually acceptable ethical standards for putting them into practice. Ethical standards consist of those principles which have been formally and publicly acknowledged by the membership of a profession to serve as guidelines governing professional conduct, discharge of duties, and resolution of moral dilemmas. In this document, the Association for Specialists in Group Work has identified the standards of conduct necessary to maintain and regulate the high standards of integrity and leadership among its members.

The Association for Specialists in Group Work recognizes the basic commitment of its members to the Ethical Standards of its parent organization, the American Personnel & Guidance Association and nothing in this document shall be construed to supplant that code. These standards are intended to complement the APGA standards in the area of group work by clarifying the nature of ethical responsibility of the counselor in the group setting and by stimulating a greater concern for competent group leadership.

The following ethical guidelines have been organized under three categories: the leader's responsibility for providing information about group work to clients, the group leader's responsibility for providing group counseling services to clients, and the group leader's responsibility for safeguarding the standards of ethical practice.

A. *Responsibility for Providing Information about Group Work and Group Services:*

A-1. Group leaders shall fully inform group members, in advance and preferably in writing, of the goals in the group, qualifications of the leader, and procedures to be employed.

A-2. The group leader shall conduct a pre-group interview with each prospective member for purposes of screening, orientation, and, in so far as possible, shall select group members whose needs and goals are compatible with the established goals of the group; who will not impede the group process; and whose well-being will not be jeopardized by the group experience.

A-3. Group leaders shall protect members by defining clearly what confidentiality means, why it is important, and the difficulties involved in enforcement.

A-4. Group leaders shall explain, as realistically as possible, exactly what services can and cannot be provided within the particular group structure offered.

A-5. Group leaders shall provide prospective clients with specific information about any specialized or experimental activities in which they may be expected to participate.

A-6. Group leaders shall stress the personal risks involved in any group, especially regarding potential life-changes, and help group members explore their readiness to face these risks.

---

[1]Approved by the ASGW Executive Board, November 11, 1980

A-7. Group leaders shall inform members that participation is voluntary and that they may exit from the group at any time.

A-8. Group leaders shall inform members about recording of sessions and how tapes will be used.

B. *Responsibility for Providing Group Services to Clients:*

B-1. Group leaders shall protect member rights against physical threats, intimidation, coercion, and undue peer pressure insofar as is reasonably possible.

B-2. Group leaders shall refrain from imposing their own agendas, needs, and values on group members.

B-3. Group leaders shall insure to the extent that it is reasonably possible that each member has the opportunity to utilize group resources and interact within the group by minimizing barriers such as rambling and monopolizing time.

B-4. Group leaders shall make every reasonable effort to treat each member individually and equally.

B-5. Group leaders shall abstain from inappropriate personal relationships with members throughout the duration of the group and any subsequent professional involvement.

B-6. Group leaders shall help promote independence of members from the group in the most efficient period of time.

B-7. Group leaders shall not attempt any technique unless thoroughly trained in its use or under supervision by an expert familiar with the intervention.

B-8. Group leaders shall not condone the use of alcohol or drugs directly prior to or during group sessions.

B-9. Group leaders shall make every effort to assist clients in developing their personal goals.

B-10. Group leaders shall provide between-session consultation to group members and follow-up after termination of the group, as needed or requested.

C. *Responsibility for Safeguarding Ethical Practice:*

C-1. Group leaders shall display these standards or make them available to group members.

C-2. Group leaders have the right to expect ethical behavior from colleagues and are obligated to rectify or disclose incompetent, unethical behavior demonstrated by a colleague by taking the following actions:

(*a*) To confront the individual with the apparent violation of ethical guidelines for the purposes of protecting the safety of any clients and to help the group leader correct any inappropriate behaviors.

(b) Such a complaint should be made in writing including the specific facts *and dates* of the alleged violation and all relevant supporting data. The complaint should be forwarded to:

> The Ethics Committee,
> c/o The President
> Association of Specialists in Group Work
> Two Skyline Place, Suite 400
> 5203 Leesburg Pike
> Falls Church, Virginia 22041

Sample Forms for Any Group

Standardizing forms helps you efficiently communicate with students, parents, and teachers regarding group counseling. We have included seven forms which we routinely use. You may need to alter some or all of these forms to meet the specific needs in your school. The topics covered by the forms are:

Teacher Referral
Group Membership Agreement
Parent Permission Form
Letter to Parents
Group Attendance
Group Goal Sheet
Group Evaluation

Teacher _____ Date _____

Referral for Counseling Services

I would like to refer the following students for:

   1. Individual Counseling
   2. Group Counseling
   3. Tutoring (Peer Helper)

(From the above list, please specify the most appropriate program under "Counseling Program" below.)

Student Name	Counseling Program	Reason for Referral (Be as specific as possible)

Group Membership Agreement

_____ has my permission to be in
(Name)

_____ , which meets for _____ weeks on
(Group name)

_____ from _____ to _____ beginning _____ .
(Day)   (Time)   (Time)   (Date)

_____
Teacher's Signature*

- -

I _____ agree that it is my
(Student's name)

responsibility to get any assignments I miss while in the group.

I also agree to let the counselor know if I am unable to attend any of the meetings due to tests, reports, and so forth.

_____
Student's Signature

*Teachers: After signing, please return to counselors.

Parent Permission Form

Dear _____,
                            (Parent's name)

_____ has been recommended for our *Friendship* group by
    (Student's name)

_____ . I have met with your son/daughter and explained
    (Teacher's name)

the content and nature of the group. The group consists of eight sessions, meeting once per week for 45 minutes. During these sessions we will be working on: *1) the characteristics of a friend; 2) recognizing one's strengths; 3) determining the do's and don'ts of being a good friend; 4) effective communication; 5) responsibility; and 6) handling stress.*

If you have any questions or comments, please feel free to contact me. We want you to be informed of your child's activities. Thank you for your support in our mutual goals of raising competent, healthy, and successful children.

Sincerely,

Counselor

Return to counselor (check one)

_____ My child may participate in these counseling sessions.

_____ My child may not participate in these counseling sessions.

Parent's signature _____

Group Counseling for School Counselors

Letter to Parents

Dear Parents:

The counseling program at _____ is designed
                                                        (Name of school)
to be preventive and developmental. In addition to seeing students individually and
in classroom guidance, we teach skills and information in small-group settings.

We have invited your child to become a member of the _____
group. We emphasize to students that groups are for everyone, and participating does
not indicate a problem. All students can benefit from learning how to accept responsibility, manage stress, communicate effectively, make decisions, and solve problems.
Students can learn from one another and enhance their self-concepts in a small-group setting.

Listed are the themes for each grade level, as well as the special-concerns groups.

6th-grade group:	friendship skills, stress management, self-esteem
7th-grade group:	communication skills—listening, asserting, exploring alternatives, and handling conflicts
8th-grade group:	decision making and problem solving
Family group:	for students whose parents are recently divorced, separated, or who have a new step-parent
Loss group:	for students who have recently experienced a death in their family

Group Attendance

Student	Teacher	1	2	3	4	5	6	7	8

Session Topics
1.
2.
3.
4.
5.
6.
7.
8.

Group Counseling for School Counselors

Group
Lesson
Plans

The following sections of the book are organized into four categories:

1. Group lesson plans for students which are divided into two parts—
   (a) Developmental groups and (b) Special Concerns groups. (Developmental groups focus on normal developmental issues and are appropriate for all students. Special concerns groups are concerned with specific problems/concerns such as divorce, loss, grades, new students which are not generic to all students.)

   The topics covered in the developmental lesson plans are:
   1) Understanding Yourself and Others (self-awareness, stress, motivation)
   2) Friendship
   3) Self-Concept
   4) Refusal Skills
   5) Handling Conflicts: Stand up to Bullies

   The topics covered in the special-concerns lesson plans are:
   1) Divorce
   2) Loss
   3) At Risk (academically)
   4) Pregnancy
   5) New Student

2. A nine-session personal-growth group for teachers.

3. Ideas and resources for leading parent groups.

4. An annotated bibliography of current research and resources for leading school counseling groups and a bibliography of some of the classic texts, articles, and research in this area.

DEVELOPMENTAL GROUPS

- Understanding Yourself and Others
- Friendship
- Self-Concept
- Refusal Skills
- Handling Conflict: Stand Up to Bullies

Understanding Yourself and Others

Grade Level: Upper Elementary, Middle School	
Time Required: Eight Sessions	
Author: Greg Brigman	

This eight-session group is organized into the following sessions:

Session 1: Thirty Personal Characteristics
Session 2: Stress
Session 3: Things I Like to Do
Session 4 & 5: Friendship
Session 6 & 7: Understanding Behavior
Session 8: Wrap-up and Evaluation

We recommend that you screen group participants prior to the first group session. See the section entitled "Getting Started."

It is helpful to have students keep a folder for handouts and daily journal writing. Five minutes before the group ends, ask students to write in their journals, "One thing I learned today . . . " or "I was surprised that . . . " or "I see that I need to . . . ." If you have time, students can share these sentences aloud. Since each session begins with a review of the previous meeting, journal entries help refresh students' memories.

Each session will include:

- an icebreaker

- a review of last session

- a new skill or activity

- journal writing

- summary (an "I learned . . . " statement)

Session 1: Thirty Personal Characteristics

■ *Introduction:*

Leader introduces self and welcomes the group. He or she gives an overview of the training, and how the skills and awareness gained can be used.

■ *Housekeeping and Rules:*

Leader explains the time and length of meetings and the notebook for journal writing.

The leader asks, "What kind of rules do you think we need for a group like this one?" Students will come up with good rules. Limit them to three or four, making sure that the following rules are included in some form:

1. Take turns speaking.

2. Don't put anyone down.

3. What you say in this room is confidential.

■ *Icebreaker:*

Have the group divide into dyads (pairs) and allow students five minutes to get acquainted with their partners. Partners will introduce each other to the group, telling about their interests and hobbies and information that was shared.

■ *Skill-Building or Awareness Activity:*

1. Hand out the reproducible "How I See Myself—30 Characteristics" activity sheets. Give students five to ten minutes to circle their responses. Then have the students write a short paragraph that explains how they see themselves.

2. Next, divide students into dyads and have partners share with each other how it felt to do this activity and how they see themselves.

3. Discuss these questions with the whole group:

   How did you feel when you did this activity?
   (Students will usually say it felt awkward or embarrassing to grade or judge themselves. Give them permission to grade themselves honestly, to give themselves high scores when they feel that way.)

   Why does it feel different to give ourselves credit?
   (Usually we have been taught not to brag, and doing this activity makes you feel as if you are bragging.)

   Which ones were hardest to do?
   ("Attractive" and "Popular" are frequent answers.)

4. Finally, have students complete the processing of the "How I See Myself" sheets using the reproducible "Processing the 30 Characteristics" activity sheet. Use this sheet to discuss the activity. You may want to have students share answers in pairs, then ask for volunteers to share with whole group.

■ *Journal Writing:*

Allow students five minutes to record their impressions of today's session.

■ *Summary:*

Ask students to complete, in their journals, the statement "Today I learned . . . . "

How I See Myself—30 Characteristics

Rate yourself on a scale from 1 to 5 on the following 30 characteristics. The 5 means you have a lot of that characteristic. The 1 means you have none, and the 3 means about average.

Go with your first impression and be honest. There are no right or wrong answers or good or bad characteristics.

No one will see this list but you unless you want to show it to someone.

	Not at All		Average		Very Much
1. Happy	1	2	3	4	5
2. Athletic	1	2	3	4	5
3. Follower	1	2	3	4	5
4. Responsible	1	2	3	4	5
5. Enthusiastic	1	2	3	4	5
6. Creative (artistically or in problem solving)	1	2	3	4	5
7. Intelligent	1	2	3	4	5
8. Good Listener	1	2	3	4	5
9. Aggressive	1	2	3	4	5
10. Friendly	1	2	3	4	5
11. Optimistic	1	2	3	4	5
12. A Leader	1	2	3	4	5
13. Shy	1	2	3	4	5
14. Helpful	1	2	3	4	5
15. A Loner	1	2	3	4	5
16. Competitive	1	2	3	4	5
17. Clumsy	1	2	3	4	5
18. Sincere	1	2	3	4	5
19. Good Sense of Humor	1	2	3	4	5
20. Outgoing	1	2	3	4	5

(continued)

Group Counseling for School Counselors

How I See Myself—30 Characteristics *(continued)*

	Not at All		Average		Very Much
21. Carefree	1	2	3	4	5
22. Open (willing to share feelings and thoughts)	1	2	3	4	5
23. Attractive	1	2	3	4	5
24. Worried	1	2	3	4	5
25. Like to Be Part of a Group	1	2	3	4	5
26. Popular	1	2	3	4	5
27. Angry	1	2	3	4	5
28. Dependable	1	2	3	4	5
29. Bored	1	2	3	4	5
30. Confident	1	2	3	4	5

Now write a short paragraph explaining how you see yourself.

Name _____ Date _____

Processing the 30 Characteristics

1. I learned I was more _____ , _____ , and

   _____ than I thought and less _____ ,

   _____ , and _____ than I thought.

2. Write a summary sentence about yourself using what you learned from reviewing
   your ratings. You may want to begin with:

   I'm the kind of person who is _____

   _____

   _____

   _____

3. Three strengths I have are: _____ , _____ ,

   and _____ .

4. The qualities I would like to have more of are: _____ ,

   _____ , and _____ .

5. With a partner, share some strengths and qualities you'd like more of.

   _____

   _____

   _____

   _____

6. Each person share this with the group: I was surprised that _____

   _____

   _____

   _____

   _____

Session 2: Stress

■ *Icebreaker:*

Have each student in turn tell the group, "My name is . . . and something I enjoy doing is . . . . "

■ *Review:*

Have students share what they learned in last week's session.

■ *Skill-Building or Awareness Activity:*

Introduce the topic of stress with the following activity.

How many of you feel some stress today?

How do you know when you are under stress? What are the symptoms? Name some physical symptoms. Think about the things that cause you stress. Imagine tossing all those words into the center of our circle in a pile. Tell us what causes you stress and throw them on the pile. (Some answers that are typically given:)

grades	boys/girls
friends	relationships
teachers	school
parents	decisions
time	tests
goals	

(As students call out different answers, have them explain how that topic causes stress.)

Sometimes we feel stress when we think we have to be perfect, expecting perfection of ourselves or others. We may feel disappointed or angry when we feel we have to perform and we don't have the resources for it.

Let's look at some ways to handle stress. (Hand out the reproducible activity sheet "Getting a Handle on Stress.")

As you read the 11 suggestions for dealing with stress:

1. Choose your favorites.

2. Check the ones you already use.

3. Circle the ones you would like to use more.

(Have volunteers read each suggestion, using each one as a stimulus to generate student discussion. Have students share their ratings and ask for examples.)

■ *Journal Writing:*

Allow students five minutes to record their impressions of today's session.

■ *Summary:*

Ask students to complete, in their journals, the statement "Today I learned . . . . "

Name _____ Date _____

Getting a Handle on Stress

1. **Work off stress.** If you are angry or upset, try to blow off steam physically by activities such as running or sports. Even taking a walk can help.

2. **Talk out your worries.** It helps to share worries with someone you trust and respect. This may be a friend, family member, teacher, or counselor. Sometimes another person can help you see a new side to your problem and, thus, a new solution.

3. **Learn to accept what you cannot change.** If the problem is beyond your control at this time, try your best to accept it until you can change it. It beats spinning your wheels and getting nowhere.

4. **Get enough sleep and rest.** Lack of sleep can lessen your ability to deal with stress by making you more irritable.

5. **Balance work and recreation.** "All work and no play can make Jack a nervous wreck!" Schedule time for recreation to relax your mind.

6. **Do something for others.** Sometimes when you are distressed, you concentrate too much on yourself and your situation. When this happens, it is often wise to do something for someone else and get your mind off yourself. There is an extra bonus in this technique: it helps to make friends.

7. **Take one thing at a time.** Many times we set ourselves up for failure by trying to do too many things at the same time. It is defeating to tackle all your tasks at once. Instead, set some aside and work on the most urgent tasks first.

8. **Give in once in a while.** If you find the source of your stress is other people, try giving in instead of fighting and insisting you are always right. You may find that others will begin to give in, too.

9. **Know your abilities and your limitations.** Many times stress is caused by asking yourself to do something you are not able to do. Before agreeing to do something you do not have to do, ask yourself if the task is within your ability to accomplish.

10. **Organize yourself and your time.** Learn ways to help yourself keep up with what you have to do. Plan how you will accomplish the necessary work. Organization can help you avoid wasting time and energy.

11. **Avoid being a perfectionist.** No one person can be perfect at everything. Do your best, but don't be afraid of making a mistake. Everyone makes mistakes, and many times we learn by our mistakes.

Adapted from "Plain Talk About Stress," DHHS Publication No. (ADM) 81-502, and Linda Worley's "The Stress Group." Cobb County Schools, Georgia.

Session 3: Things I Like to Do

■ *Icebreaker:*

Have each student in turn tell the group, "My name is . . . and how I feel on a scale of 1 to 10 is . . . ." (1 is the pits and 10 means wonderful.) Also, have each student name something he or she has done for fun in the past week.

■ *Review:*

Ask students to tell you some things they remember from your last meeting.

■ *Skill-Building or Awareness Activity:*

1. Tell students you'd like them to think about all the things they enjoy doing. Hand out the reproducible activity sheet, "Things I Like to Do." Let students spend about five minutes listing as many activities as they can.

2. After students have listed the things they enjoy doing, ask them to do the following:

   ● In the first column, check your five favorite activities.

   ● In the second column, put a *P* beside those activities you like to do with people and an *A* if you like to do that activity alone.

   ● In the third column, put a $ sign if the activity costs $5 or more each time you do that activity.

   ● In the next column, indicate by a *W* or *M* whether you have done this activity in the past week or month. If you haven't done this activity in a month, leave it blank.

   ● Now fill in the lines at the bottom of the activity sheet.

3. When students have finished marking their activity sheets, complete the activity as follows:

   ● Go around the circle and have students share the top three things they like to do.

   ● Ask how many students found that they enjoy doing more activities with people than alone.

   ● How many students had at least five or more activities that don't cost $5 each time they do them? What were these activities?

   ● How many of the activities have students done within the last week?

   ● Ask students to share with the group what they wrote at the bottom of the activity sheet about being surprised and learning about themselves.

The purpose of this activity is for students to be aware of their degree of involvement in positive activities. The more you are involved in positive pursuits that are fun and exciting, the better you feel and the less likely you are to become involved in self-destructive behaviors.

■ *Journal Writing:*

Allow students five minutes to record their impressions of today's session.

■ *Summary:*

Ask students to complete, in their journals, the statement "Today I learned . . . ." Ask volunteers to share their statements with the group.

Name _____ Date _____

Things I Like to Do

    List as many things as you can that you really enjoy doing, that are fun, that make you happy. These can be very simple or complicated; they can be done with people or alone.

1.					
2.					
3.					
4.					
5.					
6.					
7.					
8.					
9.					
10.					
11.					
12.					
13.					
14.					
15.					
16.					
17.					
18.					
19.					
20.					

What did you find out about yourself? I learned that _____

_____

_____

I was surprised (or pleased) that _____

_____

_____

Session 4: Friendship

■ *Icebreaker:*

The name game. Go around the circle with students saying their first name and an animal they like. After the first person, the second person says, "That's Tom, he likes gorillas; I'm Venetta and I like horses." Each person begins with the first person and says the name and animal of all persons before him or her.

■ *Review:*

Ask students to tell you some things they remember from your last meeting.

■ *Skill-Building or Awareness Activity:*

Hand out the reproducible activity sheet "Friendship" and have students complete it. Processing students' written responses is the heart of this session. Complete one section, then discuss.

■ *Journal Writing:*

Allow students five minutes to record their impressions of today's session.

■ *Summary:*

Ask students to complete, in their journals, the statement "Today I learned . . . . "

Remind students that this is the halfway point of the group sessions, with just four to go.

Name _____ Date _____

Friendship

1. On the back of this page, draw a picture of your best friend and write next to the picture some qualities that make that person a good friend. Share your picture with the group and tell why your friend is such a good friend.

2. Finish this sentence: "A friend is _____

_____

_____

_____

_____

_____ ."

Write as many qualities as you can think of.

3. Brainstorm and list below and on the board, "What a good friend does," and "What a good friend does not do."

Do's	Don'ts

Session 5: Friendship

■ *Icebreaker:*

Have students complete the following open-ended sentences in their journals and share with the group.

> I like being with people who . . . .
>
> I trust people who . . . .
>
> I'm a good friend because . . . .

■ *Review:*

Ask students to tell you some things they remember from your last meeting. If you didn't get a chance to finish the do's and don'ts, now is the time.

■ *Skill-Building or Awareness Activity:*

Hand out the reproducible activity sheet "Making Friends." Have students write their answers to the first part, then discuss their responses. Proceed with the other parts one at a time.

■ *Journal Writing:*

Allow students five minutes to record their impressions of today's session. Also ask them to rate their energy, mood, what they've eaten, and how much sleep/rest they've gotten, each on a 1–10 scale (10 is the best).

■ *Summary:*

Ask students to complete, in their journals, the statement "One thing I learned or relearned today was . . . " and share with the group.

Name _____   Date _____

Making Friends

1. Think about a friend you have now or used to have. Recall when, where, and

   how you met. _____

   _____

   _____

   Share your story with the group. Be sure to include what you did to help develop
   the friendship.

2. Check the boxes that are next to the techniques you like for meeting people,
   making friends, and keeping friends. Circle the boxes that are next to the techniques that are hardest for you.

   ☐ Smile. Smiling can do more to communicate that you are friendly and
   approachable than almost any other thing you can do.

   ☐ Listen. Being a good listener is very important. Listening says "I care" and
   makes the person feel important. Listening takes concentration and energy,
   but it's worth it.

   ☐ Introduce yourself. Usually others are just as cautious as you about starting a
   conversation. Most of the time they will be glad you got things started.

   ☐ Remember names and use them often.

   ☐ Spend time at places where people with some of your interests go. Spending
   time with people doing things you both enjoy builds friendship.

   ☐ Invite people to do things with you. Try to match what you like with people
   who like the same kinds of activities. Try short time periods first to find out if
   you enjoy spending time together.

   ☐ Be a complimenter. Give honest compliments. A phony compliment can lead
   to trouble. Letting people know you admire and appreciate something about
   them builds good will and shows you care.

   ☐ Share the talk time. Shoot for a 50/50 talk-listen ratio. Nobody likes the non-
   stop talker. Not talking isn't helpful either—people wonder if you're interested
   or care.

   ☐ Give parties. Invite people you think might be interesting. Ask the people you
   know to invite one of their friends.

   ☐ Get involved in after-school clubs or activities.

Sessions 6 and 7: Understanding Behavior

■ *Icebreaker:*

Ask students to raise their hand if they:

- sometimes clown around in class
- ever hide or act quiet so they won't get called on in class
- sometimes give up when they think they don't know how to do their schoolwork
- have ever threatened someone
- like it when someone pays them a compliment
- like to have their parents praise them for something they do
- like it when their teacher writes something positive on their paper
- like it when their parent lets them make a decision about something
- feel good when friends include them in an activity

■ *Review:*

Have students tell you some things they remember from your last session.

■ *Skill-Building or Awareness Activity:*

1. Introduce the lesson. Ask students:

   "How many of you like to play detective?"
   "How many of you like to figure things out?"
   "Do you think that figuring out why people act the way they do can be pretty tough without some clues?"

2. Explain to students that they can use the following three clues to take the mystery out of behavior.

   a. Behavior can follow a *pattern* or *cycle*:

      - Everybody wants to *belong*.
      - When we don't feel as if we belong, we get *discouraged*.
      - When we get discouraged, we can get *confused* about how to fit in and belong.
      - What we need in order to get back on the right track is some *encouragement*.

   b. All misbehavior has a *purpose*. The four main purposes or payoffs of misbehavior are:

      - attention
      - power
      - revenge
      - giving up

   List these goals on the chalkboard.

c. You can tell what goal a person is pursuing by looking at the *feelings* of people around that person.

These are some feelings that go with the different goals:

- Attention—irritation, annoyance
- Power—anger, frustration
- Revenge—hurt
- Giving up—hopelessness, frustration

List these feelings next to the goals on the chalkboard.

3. Have students practice identifying the goals of misbehavior:

"Now you have some clues. Let's see how good a detective you are."

Read the following five stories aloud to the group. After each story the students identify the goal of the behavior. Ask students to consider what feelings they would have around a person like this. Guide students to relate these feelings to the four goals of misbehavior you just listed on the board.

You can make copies of the story sheets to hand out to students. Have the students fill in the goal of the behavior for each story. Goals are:

- The Comedian—attention
- Pushy Bill—power
- Last-Place Paul—attention
- What's Her Name?—giving up
- Secrets—revenge

4. After the students have identified the goal(s) for the stories, discuss the questions that follow each story.

Journal Writing:

Allow students five minutes to record their impressions of today's session.

Summary:

Ask students to complete, in their journals, the statement, "Today I learned . . . ."

Note: The time required for this activity is usually two 50-minute sessions. It is especially helpful to have students discuss ways to encourage others who operate under one or more of the four mistaken goals (attention, power, revenge, giving up).

Encourage students to apply what they are learning in group to their life outside of group. Remind them that there are only two more meetings.

Why Do They Act That Way?

— The Comedian —

Pete liked to make people laugh. Most people enjoyed his clowning and joking, including the teacher. The problem was that Pete clowned all the time, whether it was appropriate or not.

During a class discussion, Pete began to clown around, disrupting the discussion. Everyone laughed. Everyone but the teacher, that is. She reminded Pete that this was not the time for joking. He quieted down for a minute or two, but then he saw another opportunity to joke, and joke he did! The teacher reminded him again.

This went on four more times during the period: joke-reminder-joke-reminder.

■ **Goal:** _____

Questions

1. Why does Pete clown around? What does he get out of this behavior?

2. What are some positive ways Pete could get attention?

— Pushy Bill —

Bill would interrupt conversations and finish the answers for others. Many times his classmates did not get their turns to talk because Bill had to tell the answer in his big, booming voice. He often whispered directions to other kids during study time, telling them what they should or should not do.

Bill pushed and shoved his playmates out of the way so he could be first in line. He often argued when his friends said something. During a discussion, Bill would always feel he was right and had to have his way or be the winner in games. Many times, Bill became very cross if he couldn't be the most important one in the group.

■ **Goal:** _____

Questions

1. What do you think about Bill?

2. What was Bill trying to do?

3. Why do you suppose he did this?

4. Is it important for Bill to be first all the time?

5. Could Bill get power some other way? How?

(continued)

Name _____ Date _____

Why Do They Act That Way? *(continued)*

— Last-Place Paul —

Paul was never in a hurry to go anyplace. Whether it was to lunch or to gym, Paul was always last to leave the room. He moved only if the teacher or another student reminded him. "Oh, come on, Paul. Hurry up!" "Oh!" he would reply, and slowly get out of his seat. "Step on it!" the teacher would command, and Paul would increase his speed a bit.

When assignments were handed in, Paul always turned his in last. Even then he only did it when the teacher said, "Paul, where's your assignment?"

■ *Goal:* _____

Questions:

1. What you think of Paul's slow behavior?

2. What happens when Paul moves slowly?

3. What are other ways students get attention by doing nothing?

4. What do you think a teacher can do if someone behaves like Paul?

5. How could we show Paul that he is an important person and that he doesn't have to drag his feet to get attention?

6. How is this story different from the previous attention story?

— What's Her Name? —

Carol was so quiet and shy that you would hardly know she was in the classroom. She always took her usual seat in the back of the room, close to the wall. As she moved toward her seat, Carol hung her head down to avoid eye contact with anyone. She rarely spoke to the other students or to the teacher—only if she couldn't avoid speaking.

Carol was particularly nervous this morning. It was the middle of the second week of school and so far she had been lucky. Ms. Jordan hadn't asked her any questions in class discussion. But Carol was afraid her luck might run out, that today might be the day. She thought to herself, "I just don't know what I'll do if she asks me a question. I don't understand this stuff. I'm too dumb to learn this anyway!"

Ms. Jordan began the discussion. "Let's see, I still haven't learned all your names. The girl in the back, next to the wall . . . " Ms. Jordan glanced at a seating chart where students had put their names next to the seats they had chosen. "Carol, isn't it? Tell me, Carol, what is the answer to number one?"

(continued)

Why Do They Act That Way? *(continued)*

Carol froze with fear, as if she were having a nightmare. "Carol, do you know the answer?" asked Ms. Jordan in a kind way. Carol sank into the chair and just shrugged her shoulders. Ms. Jordan looked uncomfortable and said, "Uh, okay, how about you, Roy?"

After that, Carol's troubles were over. Ms. Jordan didn't call on her anymore. She was safe. No one would know how dumb she felt she was.

■ *Goal:* _____

Questions:

1. What does Carol think of herself?

2. Is it possible she's not really dumb, but just thinks she is?

3. What kinds of things might convince people they are dumb even though they have average or above-average intelligence?

4. When do you feel as if you're dumb?

5. What can you tell yourself at times likes that?

6. How could we help a student who feels inadequate?

— Secrets —

Heather told her friend Sara a big secret. Sara went around telling everyone the secret, so Heather hid Sara's gym clothes and Sara got a zero for not dressing out.

■ *Goal:* _____

Questions:

1. How many of you have ever had a friend who told a secret?

2. What did you do?

3. How do you feel after getting revenge?

4. What is another way that Heather could have handled the situation?

For more information on goals of misbehavior and positive behavior, see:

Dinkmeyer, *STET—Systematic Training for Effective Teaching*
Walton, *Winning Teenagers Over*
Georgia Department of Education, *Psychological Education*

*Stories are taken from *Psychological Education: Middle School Seminar Series,* Georgia Department of Education.

Session 8: Wrap-up and Evaluation

■ *Icebreaker:*

Go around the circle, asking students to finish this sentence: "Something I would not change about myself is . . . "

■ *Review:*

Students review last meeting. Go over briefly each topic you've covered since the group began, asking for what they remember.

■ *Skill-Building or Awareness Activity:*

Accepting and Giving Compliments

1. Hand out index cards or sheets of paper. Each person is to write down at least one thing they like or appreciate about each of the other group members.

2. Spotlight: Each group member will say directly to the "spotlighted" person, with eye contact: "(*person's name*), one thing I like or appreciate about you is _____." After each comment the spotlighted person simply says thank you—nothing else. (Be sure you get in on this. It feels good.)

3. Process the spotlighting activity. How did it feel receiving compliments? Giving compliments?

4. Students complete anonymous evaluation.

Summary:

Concluding remarks. Invite students to make individual appointments if they want.

Friendship Group

Grade Level: Upper Elementary
Time Required: Six Sessions
Author: Gwendolyn Baity Cheatham

This six-session group developed after a request from a parent who felt her child would benefit from a group experience. A survey of the fifth-grade teachers revealed the same need for other students as well. The fifth-grade teachers were asked to refer two students who they felt would profit from a friendship group. After permission slips were signed by the parents of the participants, we started what has become one of our most successful and popular groups.

■ *Group Objectives:*

The group members will:

1. Analyze how people make friends.

2. Identify the most important qualities in a friend.

3. Explore the importance and responsibilities of friendship.

4. Accept that changes in friendships are natural.

5. Understand that problems are common to friendship.

6. Practice solving friendship problems.

7. Identify different types of friendship problems and explore alternative solutions.

8. Devise a plan of action for improving their friendship.

■ *Time:*

Six weekly sessions for 30 to 45 minutes.

■ *Group Composition:*

The group should consist of six to eight group members.

The activities are appropriate for fourth-, fifth-, or sixth-graders.

■ *Group Rules:*

Respect the rights of others.
No put-downs.
Don't use names when discussing a situation.
Confidentiality
Right to pass

Session 1: Friendship Group

■ *Icebreaker:*

Have the group members divide into dyads and interview each other. When the group members meet in the group, they will introduce the person they interviewed to the entire group. (Allow 5 minutes.) Write the following questions on the board as a guideline for the interviews:

Who is your teacher?

What is your hobby?

Tell me one interesting fact about you.

■ *Skill-Building or Awareness Activity:*

1. Discuss the group rules for group members.

   a. Respect the rights of others.

   b. No put-downs.

   c. No names when discussing a situation.

   d. Confidentiality.

   e. Right to pass.

2. Have the group members complete the "Friendship Quiz." Allow 10 minutes.

3. Discuss the scores with the group members.

4. Ask the group members for a thumbs-up if their answer is yes and thumbs-down if their answer is no to the following questions:

   a. How many of you have a best friend?

   b. How many of you have a friend now that you did not like before?

   c. How many of you have a good friend of the opposite sex?

   d. How many of you have had a fight or argument with a friend recently?

   e. How many of you have a brother or sister who is also your friend?

Allow and encourage members to elaborate on any of the questions.

■ *Summary:*

Close the session with expectations for the group. "I hope to learn . . . . "

■ *Materials:*

Friendship Quiz, pencil, blackboard and chalk.

Name _____ Date _____

Friendship Quiz

Answer the following questions as honestly as you can. You are the only one who will see your score on this quiz. Circle one answer for each question, using the following scale:

1 – Never   2 – Sometimes   3 – Most of the time   4 – Always

1 2 3 4	1. I enjoy meeting new people.
1 2 3 4	2. I am able to remember people's names.
1 2 3 4	3. I can carry on a conversation with someone I have just met.
1 2 3 4	4. I am considerate (thoughtful) of other people's feelings.
1 2 3 4	5. I enjoy group activities.
1 2 3 4	6. I am able to control my temper.
1 2 3 4	7. I am able to laugh at myself.
1 2 3 4	8. I am able to find something to like in most people.
1 2 3 4	9. I try to talk with a friend who has let me down.
1 2 3 4	10. I avoid arguments with friends.
1 2 3 4	11. I get along well with many types of people.
1 2 3 4	12. I avoid criticizing friends.
1 2 3 4	13. People seem to enjoy doing things with me.
1 2 3 4	14. I belong to at least one group activity, such as sports, clubs, church groups, etc.
1 2 3 4	15. I try to find ways to compliment friends.
1 2 3 4	16. I am glad when my friends make new friends.
1 2 3 4	17. I avoid gossiping or talking about people.
1 2 3 4	18. I act the same toward my friends when I'm with different groups of people.
1 2 3 4	19. I am a good listener.
1 2 3 4	20. I am able to keep a secret.
1 2 3 4	21. I can be counted on to do what I say I will do.
1 2 3 4	22. I am able to say "I'm sorry" when I make a mistake.
1 2 3 4	23. I avoid telling others what they should and should not do.
1 2 3 4	24. I am able to forgive others when they make a mistake.
1 2 3 4	25. I try to show my friends they are important to me.

(continued)

Friendship Quiz *(continued)*

To Score Yourself—Add the total of all the numbers you circled. The highest possible score is 100.

75–100   You probably already have many friends and are able to get along well with them most of the time.

50–74   Like many people, you probably have the potential to make and keep many friends, but right now you may be having some problems in some of your friendships.

25–49   You have much room for improvement in your ability to make and keep friends.

Getting to Know You and the People in Your Life by Linda Pace Worley. J. Weston Walch, Publisher, 1985. (No longer in print.)

Session 2: Friendship Group

■ *Icebreaker:*

Group members will sit in a circle and think of one adjective to describe themselves that begins with the same letter of their first name. As they rotate around the circle, they must repeat the names and adjectives of the group members before them. (Example: lovely Lynn, exciting Erin.)

■ *Review:*

Summarize last week's session by asking: "Who remembers what we did the last time we met?"

■ *Skill-Building or Awareness Activity:*

1. Have the group members close their eyes and think of someone who is or was their friend. After about 25 seconds, ask for volunteers to tell about their friend, how they met, and what they do together.

2. Ask group members to brainstorm some important qualities of friendship. Write their answers on the board. Discuss each attribute and then have the group members decide what three qualities are most important.

■ *Summary:*

Close the session by having the group members complete the sentence, "A friend is . . . ."

■ *Materials:*

Blackboard or chart; chalk or pen.

Session 3: Friendship Group

■ *Icebreaker:*

Members will pull a sentence stem from a hat and complete the sentence. The sentences deal with friendship. (Example: My first friend . . . , Friends are important because . . . , Making friends is . . . , When I'm with friends I like to . . . .)

■ *Review:*

Summarize last week's session by asking the students to recall the three qualities that they had decided were the most important in friendship.

■ *Skill-Building or Awareness Activity:*

1. The group leader should write the following slogans on the board and lead a discussion on the meaning and importance of each:

   a. Be a friend to yourself.

   b. Be cheerful.

   c. Go where people are.

   d. Be yourself.

   e. Don't expect perfection in your friends.

   f. Friendship is give-and-take.

   g. Give your friend space.

   h. A friend is a present you give yourself.

   i. It's smart to pick your friends . . . but not to pieces!

   j. Recipe for having friends: be one!

   k. One does not make friends; one recognizes them.

   l. Bury the faults of a friend in a fair-sized cemetery.

2. Divide the group into dyads and have each dyad develop a friendship slogan. (Allow 10 minutes.)

■ *Summary:*

In closing, allow each dyad to present their slogan to the other group members.

■ *Materials:*

Paper; pencils; blackboard or chart; chalk or pen.

Session 4: Friendship Group

■ *Icebreaker:*

Ask the members to complete the following sentence: "I show that I like my friends when I . . . . "

■ *Review:*

Have the group members recall the friendship slogans developed during last week's session.

■ *Skill-Building or Awareness Activity:*

1. Show the filmstrip, *Friends: How They Help . . . How They Hurt.* Part I opens with an explanation of why friendships are likely to change. Although losing a friend is painful, it is part of growing up.

2. Discuss the filmstrip with the group members.

3. In part II, the students are given the chance to practice solving friendship problems. The situations presented in the filmstrip involve loyalty, peer pressure, responsibility, and alcohol abuse. Discussion questions follow each situation.

■ *Summary:*

Close the session by asking the group members to complete the sentence, "I learned . . . . "

■ *Materials:*

Filmstrip; tape; projector; screen.
Friends: How They Help . . . How They Hurt
Sunburst Communications, Inc.
Pleasantville, N.Y. 10570   1985
(Set contains two filmstrips and two cassettes.)

Session 5: Friendship Group

■ *Icebreaker:*

Imagine that a new student has enrolled in your school. You want to be that person's friend. How will you let that person know?

■ *Review:*

Review last week's session by asking, "Who remembers what we did last week?"

■ *Skill-Building or Awareness Activity:*

1. Have the students write down problems that they have encountered in their friendships. (Allow about 5 minutes.)

2. Read problems aloud and lead the students in a discussion of some possible solutions.

3. Divide the group into dyads and have them role-play the problem and an alternative solution. (Allow 5 minutes practice time.)

■ *Summary:*

Close the session by having the group members describe one way that they have been a good friend in the last week.

■ *Materials:*

Paper; pencils.

Session 6: Friendship Group

■ *Icebreaker:*

Ask the group members to complete the sentence, "A friend is someone who . . . . "

■ *Review:*

Ask the members to share an experience they had during the week in which they used the methods role-played from last week.

■ *Skill-Building or Awareness Activity:*

1. The group will write advertisements for a school newspaper. It will be titled, "Wanted!" The ad should describe why the group member would be a good friend.

2. Allow group members to share their advertisements.

3. Have each group member come up with a plan of action for improving his/her friendships.

4. Set a date one month away for the group members to reconvene to talk about the success or failure of their plans and to make appropriate revisions.

5. Distribute group evaluation forms for group members to complete.

■ *Summary:*

Add closure to the session by asking, "What is different about your friendship now from the way it was in the beginning?"

■ *Materials:*

Paper; markers; crayons; group evaluation forms; pencils.

Resources

Friends: How They Help . . . How They Hurt
Sunburst Communications, Inc.
Pleasantville, N.Y. 10570
1985
(Set contains two filmstrips and two cassettes.)

Chase, Larry, *The Other Side of the Report Card*, Goodyear Publishing Company, Inc., 1976. Pacific Palisades, California 90272

Friendship Group

Grade Level: Middle School	
Time Required: Eight Sessions	
Author: Greg Brigman	

Over my years of school counseling, I have found peer-related problems to be among the top concerns of young people. Several beliefs led me to create this group plan:

1. Feeling included or a sense of belonging is vitally important.

2. Kids experiencing difficulties with peers often have deficits in awareness and skills needed for effective relationships.

3. Even the most "normal" kids can grow in their ability to initiate and maintain satisfying friendships.

I have experimented with scores of activities and approaches to this topic. The following is my latest, but I am sure not my last, plan for this developmental area.

■ Group Objectives:

1. To identify the characteristics of a friend.

2. To recognize one's strengths.

3. To become aware of areas one would like to improve in order to have more satisfying relationships.

4. To determine the "Do's and Don'ts" of being a good friend.

5. To learn specific encouragement skills for self and others.

■ Length of Time:

Once per week, 45–50 minutes, for eight weeks.

■ Group Composition:

Six to ten students with varying levels of peer-relations skills as determined by teacher and parent recommendations and counselor evaluation. It is important to have a few students who have good peer relations for the purpose of positive role modeling.

■ *Group Rules:*

1. Confidentiality
2. Right to pass
3. One person speaks at a time—the rest of us listen.
4. No put-downs.
5. Share the time—no monopolizing talk time.

Session 1: Friendship Group

Collect the parent permission forms and take roll.

■ *Introduction:*

Introduce yourself and explain the purpose of the group. Example: "This is a friendship group, and the purpose is for us to explore the topic of friendship. Would you agree that friendship is an important topic for people? How many think there may be something you don't know about friendship? I don't think we ever know it all; but this group will give us a chance to hear and talk about what you look for in a friend, ways to meet new friends, how friends help and hurt, and some do's and don'ts of being a good friend. This group meets eight times, same time, same place, every week. As I mentioned when I met with each of you individually, there are three ways people get to participate in this group: 1) you heard about the group and thought it sounded good and signed up; 2) your parent heard or read about it and wanted you to check it out; 3) your teacher thought you'd enjoy it and that you'd be able to benefit by being in the group.

"As you probably know, this group is open to everyone. You don't have to have a problem with friends to be here. But if you're like most of us, you occasionally run into a tough spot with some of your friends, or with people you'd like to get along with better. Anyway, however you got here, I'm glad you're here. As you all know, this is a voluntary group—no one has to be here. Each of you has agreed to come to all eight meetings. I will tell you that about 9 of 10 students who do come to all the meetings report, on an anonymous evaluation we give at the end, that they enjoyed it, they learned some things, and they would recommend it to a friend."

■ *Icebreaker:*

Go around the circle asking students to say their names and one thing they enjoy doing. (My name is . . . and I enjoy . . . .)

■ *Housekeeping:*

Go over the group membership agreement and have the students fill in their parts and sign. Ask them to have the teacher whose class they will miss sign the form and then return the form to you before the next meeting.

■ *Group Rules:*

Ask, "What are some rules you think would help our group run better? I've found it's helpful to have a few rules to make our group run smoothly." Make sure to include the following:

1. Anything we talk about here is confidential—we do not talk about it outside the group.

2. You have a right to say "pass" if you do not want to share your opinion on something. We do not want to make anyone uncomfortable.

3. One person talks at a time—the rest of us listen.

4. No put-downs.

5. Share the time—no monopolizing "talk time."

Ask for additional suggestions—get a group consensus on all rules.

■ *Skill-Building or Awareness Activity:*

Statistical Treasure Hunt

Divide the larger group into groups of 3 or 4, and assign a reporter for each group. After the groups finish the "Statistical Treasure Hunt," go through each item and determine which group had the most points. The winning team gets a trip to Hawaii.

■ *Summary:*

Ask students what the purpose of the group is, how many meetings, and so forth. Remind them about the agreement sheet. Preview the second meeting.

■ *Materials:*

"Statistical Treasure Hunt" handout; group membership agreement.

Name _____ Date _____

Statistical Treasure Hunt

Divide the group into teams of equal number, if possible. Give each team the questions listed below. More can be added if you desire. The questions are to be answered and evaluated as indicated on the sheet. Each team appoints a captain who collects and records the information.

_____ 1. Counting January as one point, February as two points, and so on through the calendar year, add up the total number of birthday points in your group. Just ask them what month they were born, not the year.

_____ 2. Counting one point for each different state named, give a score for the different number of birth states represesented on your team.

_____ 3. Total all the shoe sizes together (one foot only).

_____ 4. Score one point for the number of schools attended.

_____ 5. Total the number in each family.

_____ 6. Total the number of pets in each house.

_____ 7. Total the number of people in your group wearing braces.

_____ 8. Score one point for every team (sports) you have been on.

_____ 9. Score one point for every book read for fun in the last two months.

_____ 10. Total the number of people who play a musical instrument.

_____ Total for your group

Session 2: Friendship Group

■ *Introduction:*

Take roll, make sure you have agreement forms from everyone. If necessary, have the students complete another and put in their teacher's mailbox.

■ *Icebreaker:*

"The Name Game." Go around the circle asking students to say their first name and an animal they like. After the first person, the second person says, "That's Tom, he likes gorillas, and I'm Mary and I like horses," and so on. Each person begins with the first person and gives the names and animals of all persons coming before. (Pay attention. The leader says all of the names and the animals at the end.) It is important to have everyone know all the names.

■ *Skill-Building or Awareness Activity:*

Draw a Friend

1. Hand out a blank sheet of paper with magic markers or pencils. Say, "Draw a picture of your best friend—now or in the past—or the friend you'd like to have, and write below the picture some qualities that make that person a good friend." (Stress the qualities, not the art—model by drawing a stick figure.) When everyone's finished, ask all of the students to show their pictures individually and tell why their friend is such a good friend. The leader goes first to model the behavior.

2. On the back of their papers, have students finish this sentence: "A friend is . . . . " Ask them to write as many qualities as they can recall.

3. When processing this exercise, ask a student to record on poster board with a magic marker the qualities the students have in common.

■ *Summary:*

Ask the students to write their answer to one of these sentence stems: One thing I learned today was . . . ; One thing I relearned today was . . . ; One thing I was surprised at was . . . .

Have the students share their answers. Then preview Session 3.

Session 3: Friendship Group

■ *Icebreaker:*

Students tell their names, how they are feeling on a scale of 1–10, and one thing they are looking forward to this week.

■ *Review:*

Ask, "Who can remember something we did last week?" Show poster board with qualities of a friend.

■ *Skill-Building or Awareness Activity:*

1. Interview—Introduction Activity.
   Divide the group into pairs. Ask them to interview each other for some basic information that they'll use to introduce each other to the rest of the group. Notes are not allowed. Students should find out the following information about their partners: name; brothers and/or sisters, including ages; if they've lived anywhere else; if they have pets; and what they like to do for fun. After getting this information they should repeat it to make sure they have it right. (Allow two minutes each.)

   After everyone is ready, the group leader introduces his/her partner to the group to model the appropriate way to do the introduction, then everyone else takes a turn. After the introduction, ask the group for things the group members have in common.

2. Do's and Don'ts of Being a Friend.
   Ask students to brainstorm at least 10 answers for "What does a good friend do, and what does a good friend *not* do." Select a student to record answers on poster board. After students name at least 10 in each category ask them to choose the top three do's and the worst three don'ts.

3. Goal Writing.
   Using the list of qualities from last week and the list of do's and don'ts from this week, students write a goal for themselves for the coming week. Ask them to include something they want to do more of and something they want to do less of. They don't have to share their goals with the group unless they want to. Those willing to share one or both goals have a chance to report.

■ *Summary:*

Ask students to complete the sentence, "One thing I learned or relearned today was . . . . " (It's helpful to ask them to write a response, then go around circle giving everyone a chance to respond.) Preview next session.

Session 4: Friendship Group

■ *Icebreaker:*

Go around the circle, asking students to share their name and something good that happened to them in the last day or two. Explain that this can be as simple as "_____ smiled at me," or "I took a nice walk."

■ *Review:*

Ask group members to share with the group their goal from last meeting, what they did to achieve it, and how it went. (As the group matures, this portion of the meeting will lengthen as more members feel free to share.)

Ask students for a summary of the last meeting, including "Do's and Don'ts" (bring out poster from last meeting to let them check their recollection of the two lists).

■ *Skill-Building or Awareness Activity:*

How I See Myself

1. Tell students: "One of the do's of being a good friend is feeling good about yourself. People who like themselves seem to be more fun and enjoyable to be with. One of the ways we learn to like ourselves is by looking at what we think about ourselves. Accepting ourselves and appreciating our good points help us be the kind of friend others would like to have.

   "To help us look at how we think about ourselves, I have this list of words. Let's take a few minutes to read each word and rate how much or how little that word describes how you see yourself." (Pass around handout "How I See Myself." Explain the meaning of each word, and/or ask for definitions.)

2. After students have finished rating all 30 adjectives, ask them to complete #1 on "Processing the 30 Characteristics." When they're ready, ask for volunteers to share what they wrote. Ask them to complete #2, #3, and #4.

3. Allow a few minutes to have them share with a partner as they do #5.

4. Go around the circle with #6.

■ *Summary:*

Ask group members to write a goal for the week that involves meeting a new friend or getting to know an acquaintance better.

Preview next meeting. Mention that they are halfway through the group. Encourage them to work hard at their goals so they'll get more out of the rest of the meetings.

How I See Myself

	Not At All		Average		Very Much
1. Happy	1	2	3	4	5
2. Athletic	1	2	3	4	5
3. Follower	1	2	3	4	5
4. Responsible	1	2	3	4	5
5. Enthusiastic	1	2	3	4	5
6. Creative	1	2	3	4	5
7. Intelligent	1	2	3	4	5
8. Good listener	1	2	3	4	5
9. Aggressive	1	2	3	4	5
10. Sad	1	2	3	4	5
11. Optimistic	1	2	3	4	5
12. A leader	1	2	3	4	5
13. Shy	1	2	3	4	5
14. Helpful	1	2	3	4	5
15. A loner	1	2	3	4	5
16. Competitive	1	2	3	4	5
17. Clumsy	1	2	3	4	5
18. Sincere	1	2	3	4	5
19. Envious	1	2	3	4	5
20. Outgoing	1	2	3	4	5
21. Discouraged	1	2	3	4	5
22. Open	1	2	3	4	5
23. Attractive	1	2	3	4	5
24. Worried	1	2	3	4	5
25. Sociable	1	2	3	4	5
26. Popular	1	2	3	4	5
27. Angry	1	2	3	4	5
28. Dependable	1	2	3	4	5
29. Bored	1	2	3	4	5
30. Confident	1	2	3	4	5

Name _____ Date _____

Processing the 30 Characteristics

1. I learned I was more _____ , _____ , and

   _____ than I thought and less _____ ,

   _____ , and _____ than I thought.

2. Write a summary sentence about yourself using what you learned from reviewing your ratings. You may want to begin with:

   I'm the kind of person who is _____

   _____

   _____

   _____

3. Three strengths I have are: _____ , _____ ,

   and _____ .

4. The qualities I would like to have more of are: _____ ,

   _____ , and _____ .

5. With a partner, share some strengths and qualities you'd like more of.

6. Each person share this with the group: I was surprised that _____

   _____

   _____

   _____

   _____

Session 5: Friendship Group

■ *Icebreaker:*

Ask students to give their name and 2–3 things they really like to do.

■ *Review:*

Students summarize the previous meeting. Check on goals.

■ *Skill-Building or Awareness Activity:*

1. Ask students to brainstorm at least 10 ways to meet new people or make new friends. (List on poster.) Ask students for some advantages and disadvantages of each method. Ask them to choose their top three methods from the list. Go through the list, asking how many students had each suggestion as one of their top three. Tally and record the number by each suggestion.

2. Role-play the top three methods, using 1) individual models to demonstrate each method, or 2) pairs of students to practice each method.

3. Ask students to choose one or more ideas from the list and try each one at least once a day between now and next week. Tell them that you will ask them to report on one of their friend-making methods.

■ *Summary:*

Ask students to complete this sentence: "One thing I learned or relearned today was . . . ."

Session 6: Friendship Group

■ *Icebreaker:*

Ask students to share their name and complete this sentence: "Something I would like to learn or try is . . . . "

■ *Review:*

Ask students, "Who can tell me something we did last week?" Ask students to share what they tried regarding meeting new people and/or making new friends.

■ *Skill-Building or Awareness Activity:*

Inviting and Disinviting Actions and Words

1. Have students remember a time when they made a new friend. What happened? What did they do or say? Have volunteers share with group.

2. Introduce the idea of encouraging and discouraging actions and words. Pass out both handouts. Ask students to put one check beside all the words or actions that they believe apply to them, and two checks beside words or actions they say or do frequently. You may want to have students role-play some words or actions from both lists, then process the messages and feelings associated with them.

3. Ask students to write a goal for the week and share it with the group.

■ *Summary:*

Ask students to summarize the content of the meeting. Ask each to respond to: "One thing I was surprised by was . . . " or "One thing I learned or relearned was . . . . "

Preview next week and mention that next week is the next-to-last meeting.

Encouraging and Discouraging Actions and Words

Encouraging Actions and Words	*Discouraging Actions and Words*

Encouraging Actions and Words

Smiling
Listening carefully
Leaning forward
Showing interest with facial expressions
"Thanks, that helped a lot."
Patting on the back
Sharing the talk time
Introducing yourself
Remembering names and using them
    often
Inviting people to do things with you
"Tell me about it."
Sharing your lunch
Giving honest compliments
"We missed you."
Accepting compliments with "thank you"
Waiting your turn
"I like that idea."
"I liked the way you handled that."
"Knowing you, I'm sure you'll do fine."
"Can I help?"
"I'm glad you're back."

Discouraging Actions and Words

"I don't care."
"That's a dumb idea."
Interrupting
Putting someone down
Laughing when someone makes a mistake
"That's stupid to feel that way."
"Anybody with half a brain could do that."
Fidgeting with your hands and feet when
    someone is talking to you
Looking away when someone is talking to
    you
"So what?"
Pushing or hitting someone
Lying
Teasing

Session 7: Friendship Group

■ *Icebreaker:*

Ask students to share their name and complete this sentence: "One thing I do pretty well is . . . ."

■ *Review:*

Students review last meeting, and report on how they are faring with their goals.

■ *Skill-Building or Awareness Activity:*

1. Introduce the lesson this way: "I'd like for us to talk about encouragement and discouragement today. I believe that when people act in unfriendly ways on a regular basis it's a sign that they are discouraged. They don't feel they are fitting in the way they want to, and so they act in certain ways to get noticed, or appear better, or appear helpless.

   "You probably all know people who try to keep the spotlight on themselves; people who try to bully or act superior; and people who act shy or helpless. I think they believe they won't be accepted if they just act like themselves, so they act in one of these ways. They need some encouragement, both from inside and outside.

   "Let's think about the inside first. Imagine someone who always wants the spotlight. What might he/she be telling himself/herself to feel discouraged?" (Nobody pays any attention to me; they think I'm a zero; I've got to keep them noticing me or I'll never fit in.) "How does this kind of behavior—attention seeking—come across to others? What messages are others getting?" (I'm a show-off; I'm stuck-up; I'm an attention hog; I like to make you mad). "This is really different from the message intended, i.e., I want to be accepted. What could be some better ways to fit in, to be accepted?

   "How about encouragement from the outside? How could we encourage people like this to drop the attention stuff and just be themselves?" (Examples: 1) Invite them to join in; 2) be honest with them: *When you talk all the time I feel angry*; 3) smile and act friendly when they aren't doing their attention number, ignore them when they are.)

2. Go through bully type and shy type, using same questions as above.

■ *Summary:*

"What have we been doing today?" Have students share responses to: "One thing I learned or relearned today was . . . ."

Preview next meeting; remind them that it's the last meeting.

Session 8: Friendship Group

■ *Icebreaker:*

Ask students to complete this sentence: "Something I would not change about myself is . . . . "

■ *Review:*

Briefly go over each topic you've covered, asking for what they remember.

■ *Skill-Building or Awareness Activity:*

Accepting and Giving Compliments

1. Hand out index cards or sheets of paper. Each person is to write down at least one thing he or she likes or appreciates about each of the other group members.

2. Spotlight: Each group member will say directly to the "spotlighted" person, with eye contact: *person's name*, one thing I like or appreciate about you is _____ . After each comment, the spotlighted person simply says thank you—nothing else. (Be sure you get in on this. It feels good.)

3. Process the spotlighting activity. How did it feel receiving compliments? Giving compliments?

4. Students complete anonymous evaluation.

■ *Summary:*

Concluding remarks. Invite students to make individual appointments if they want.

Resources

Booher, Dianna. *Making Friends with Yourself and Other Strangers*. Julian Mesner, New York, 1982.

Kalb, Jonah, and David Viscott, M.D. *What Every Kid Should Know*. Houghton Mifflin, Boston, Massachusetts, 1976.

Purkey, William. *Inviting School Success*. Wadsworth Publishing Company, Belmont, California, 1984.

Shedd, Charlie. *You Are Somebody Special*. McGraw-Hill, New York, 1982.

Varenhorst, Barbara. *Real Friends: Becoming the Friend You'd Like to Have*. Harper & Row, San Francisco, 1983.

Video or Filmstrip. *Friends: How They Help . . . How They Hurt*. Sunburst Communications, Dept. AW, 39 Washington Ave., Pleasantville, New York 10570.

Self-Concept Group

Grade Level: Elementary (K–1)	
Time Required: Six Sessions	
Author: Sherry Stahler	

The following six-session outline is geared toward children in kindergarten, readiness, and first grade. Because it targets children with low self-esteem, each week's lesson is devoted to self-exploration and the development of a positive self-concept.

Group participation may come from three different sources: parent referrals, teacher referrals, and/or self-referrals. Group members may be from different classrooms and of either gender. The group size is between five and eight students. Each session is thirty minutes long.

The actual meeting time for the group should be predetermined with both the counselor and teachers to avoid any conflict in schedules. For the first meeting, it is recommended that the counselor pick up each group member from his/her classroom and walk together to the counselor's office. This process demonstrates the appropriate route for each child to take and makes this initial session more comfortable. For the second through sixth sessions, the counselor can put a reminder in the teacher's box on the meeting day or call the children to group at the starting time.

Session 1: Self-Concept Group

■ *Objectives:*

To understand the group's purpose
To begin to build group cohesion
To understand organizational aspects of group participation

■ *Introduction:*

When the children are all seated in a circle, begin to explain that one of the counselor's jobs is to have small groups. A small group is just like what they are in now: students from different classes all meeting together for the same reason. That reason is to remember how special we all are. Ask how many members sometimes forget that they are special, or if they sometimes say, "I can't do that—it's too hard!" or "I'm stupid!" After the children nod or speak their agreement, the counselor may say, "Well, that's why we're here—to remember that we are special and that we can do lots of different things." Ask how many people want to be in the group.

■ *Icebreaker:*

Ask each child to introduce himself/herself, tell what food he/she hates, and what activity he/she loves to do. After everyone has done this, have group members see how many names they can remember.

■ *Skill-Building or Awareness Activity:*

1. Go over the small-group rules. Make sure all students understand what they mean. These rules are
   1. Everything you say or hear is confidential.
   2. Listen and help.
   3. Let one person speak at a time.
2. After that, pass out parent permission letters. Explain what these are, why they are needed, and how they need to be returned.
3. Remind children of the day and time of group meetings, how they are expected to come to group, and how to properly walk in the hall.

■ *Summary:*

End with encouraging comments about sessions to come, and dismiss.

Session 2: Self-Concept Group

■ *Objectives:*

To participate in activities which emphasize the uniqueness of oneself
To identify one's strengths and weaknesses

■ *Icebreaker:*

After the children are all seated in a circle, have a few volunteers review all members' names.

■ *Skill-Building or Awareness Activity:*

Today's activity is "charades" with a twist. To help the members see that they are all different, volunteers pantomime activities that are easy for them to do. Individuals guess what the activity might be. The person who guesses correctly goes next. Each member has two opportunities to act out his or her different strengths, and then the cycle repeats itself with tasks that are difficult for each to accomplish.

■ *Summary:*

Once all participants have had their turns, discuss how everyone is different and that what is easy for one person is hard for someone else. Explain that all people have different strengths and weaknesses and therefore are all unique.

Session 3: Self-Concept Group

■ *Objectives:*

To feel good about one's growth in capabilities

To acknowledge that those activities which were once difficult are often able to be mastered over time

■ *Icebreaker:*

Begin again by reviewing all members' names.

■ *Skill-Building or Awareness Activity:*

Today's session is a learning-experience activity, with the counselor writing what the children say. Discussion is centered around the fact that as we grow and get older, we are able to do more and more things. The mastery of new tasks is chronicled as each group member shares an activity he/she was unable to complete at yearly intervals but is currently able to do. The end refrain of each year is: "But I can do it now!" The format is as follows:

"When I was 1 year old, I could not . . . . " (Student answers are recorded on paper.) "But I can do it now!"

"When I was 2 years old, I could not . . . . " (Student answers are recorded on paper.) "But I can do it now!"

(Proceed consecutively until the current ages are reached.)

"Now that I am 5 and 6 years old, I am learning to. . . . " (Student answers are recorded on paper.)

"Things are getting easier for me to do!"

■ *Summary:*

The whole written passage is read together as a sense of pride and accomplishment is realized.

Session 4: Self-Concept Group

■ *Objectives:*

To recognize and express one's own feelings
To recognize and understand that others share similar feelings

■ *Icebreaker:*

Today I feel . . . .

■ *Skill-Building or Awareness Activity:*

Today's activity is a game that centers on emotions. Helping the members feel comfortable expressing their thoughts and feelings is what this activity is all about. On a large poster board is a circle divided into eight sections, each with a different *feeling* word. These words are: happy, embarrassed, excited, angry, sad, left out, nervous, and puzzled. Show the board to the children; review and explain each word. The game is played like a bean-bag toss: whatever feeling word is bagged, the child shares a time when he/she felt that way. Each child has three turns.

■ *Summary:*

Discuss what emotions and experiences were shared to discover similarities among people.

Session 5: Self-Concept Group

■ *Objectives:*

To feel good about oneself
To communicate with others positive perceptions of oneself

■ *Icebreaker:*

Something fun I have done this week is . . . .

■ *Review:*

Begin today's group by having the children review all that they have done and learned so far.

■ *Skill-Building or Awareness Activity:*

Tell the children that they are going to hear a wonderful story about a hippopotamus who stops being happy. It is their job to figure out why. Read *You Look Ridiculous Said the Rhinoceros to the Hippopotamus*, by Bernard Waber.

■ *Summary:*

Discuss with the children the need to love oneself, and have them share something they like about themselves. Then, to get ready for their self-portraits, have them get into partners and trace each other's upper bodies on big poster boards.

Session 6: Self-Concept Group

■ *Objectives:*

To feel good about one's looks

To communicate to others positive perceptions of them

■ *Icebreaker:*

One thing I like about the way I look is . . . .

■ *Skill-Building or Awareness Activity:*

1. For the final session, the members complete self-portraits on their poster boards traced in Session 5. When completed, they share their pictures with the group. After each picture is shown, all the other group members say something positive to that child. The counselor will probably need to model this activity.

2. As a type of evaluation, have the children answer the following questions:

What did you learn about yourself in the group?

What did you like or not like about coming to group?

What do you remember most about being in the group?

■ *Summary:*

Remind the children that even though the group is now over, if they ever need to talk with you, or if they have a problem they want some help with, they can see you again.

Resources for Self-Concept Group

Bisignano, Judy. *Relating to Myself, To People Close to Me, To People Throughout the World.* Good Apple, Inc., Carthage, Illinois, 1985.

Canfield, Jack, and Harold C. Wells. *One Hundred Ways to Enhance Self-Concept in the Classroom: a Handbook for Teachers and Parents.* Prentice-Hall, Inc., Englewood Cliffs, New Jersey, 1976.

Chase, Larry. *The Other Side of the Report Card.* Goodyear Publishing Company, Inc., Santa Monica, California, 1975.

Landy, Lois. *Child Support Through Small Group Counseling.* Lois Landy, Savannah, Georgia, 1984.

Schwartz, Linda. *I am Special.* The Learning Works, 1978.

Waber, Bernard. *You Look Ridiculous Said the Rhinoceros to the Hippopotamus.* Houghton Mifflin Co., Boston, Massachusetts, 1966.

Self-Concept Group

Grade Level: Elementary (4–5)	
Time Required: Six Sessions	
Author: Annette Hildreth	

■ *Purpose:*

The purpose of this group is for students to get to know themselves and others better, to work on a positive self-concept, and to increase interpersonal skills. During the first session, the counselor discusses the purposes with the students.

■ *Time:*

The group meets for thirty minutes once a week for six weeks. This group can regroup in six weeks and meet for another six weeks if desired.

■ *Group Composition:*

The group is composed of six to eight (usually six) members. This type of group is usually made up of students from one class, but not always. Sometimes these groups contain boys and girls, sometimes all girls, all boys. They are usually fourth- or fifth-grade students whose teachers feel that they need a little extra attention, a boost to their self-esteem.

■ *Group Rules:*

1. Be on time.

2. One person talks at a time.

3. Use a soft voice. (We're located in the front office.)

4. Be a polite listener.

5. No put downs—treat group members as you want to be treated.

The importance of confidentiality is discussed with participants. Groups meet at the same time each week; one member is assigned responsibility (this rotates) to remind group of next meeting.

Session 1: Self-Concept Group

■ *Icebreaker:*

Introduce yourself to your students; include something about yourself that they may not already know. Ask if anyone has been in a group before. Tell students the purpose of this group and mention the group rules. Ask if everyone is comfortable with this.

■ *Skill-Building or Awareness Activity:*

Partner Interview

1. Break students into pairs (preferably not with someone they know well) and assign them to different parts of room, out in hall, etc. Set time limit for each interview and give suggestions for possible questions. Examples: Where were you born? Where have you lived? What's your favorite TV show? What do you like to do best? Tell something about your family.

2. After interviews are done, have students regroup and introduce each other. (A shy child finds this easier than introducing himself/herself.) After each introduction, the group may ask further questions if there is something they would like to know.

■ *Summary:*

When introductions are over, ask: What did you learn about each other that you didn't know? How did it feel to hear yourself introduced? Close with the following sentence stem: "I think being in this group will be . . . ." (Ask for *one* word: this is hard, students usually want to add more.)

Session 2: Self-Concept Group

■ *Icebreaker and Review:*

Open by recalling last week when they all introduced each other. Ask them to rate how comfortable they feel starting this session on a 1–5 scale, with 5 being very comfortable. Go around group with this and discuss briefly.

■ *Skill-Building or Awareness Activity:*

1. In this session, objectives are to increase students' comfort level with each other by letting them get to know more about each other (and themselves); to find similarities and also differences; to find that differences are OK.

2. "Corners" activity.

■ *Instructions to students:*

Take a piece of paper and fold it in four parts; write your name in the middle of the paper. In the upper right-hand corner of the paper, write the word FAVORITES and numbers 1–3. Write answers to the following questions:

1. Song

2. Thing—what would you grab if your house caught on fire (assuming pets and people are safe)?

3. Outdoor activity

Fill in the remaining three sections as follows:

■ *Places (in upper left-hand corner)*

1. A place where you can relax and feel comfortable

2. A place where you would vacation if you could

3. A place where you would move to if you could

■ *People (in lower left-hand corner)*

1. A person who makes you feel safe and comfortable

2. A person you admire and respect

3. Someone you would like to know better

■ *School (in lower right-hand corner)*

1. Subject you like best

2. One thing you would change about your classroom

3. A teacher or staff member who has been helpful

After the four corners are filled, the group can proceed in two different ways. 1) Students can take a partner, discuss a corner, change partners, discuss next corner, etc. 2) Leader may say, "This is how I filled in number one in 'favorites'; who would like to tell what they put for number two?" and continue that way.

■ *Summary:*

Discuss the activity. What was it like? What did you learn about yourself and others? (Example: I learned that Kim and I like the same song.) Again, ask for comfort rating 1–5 and discuss changes from beginning if any.

■ *Materials:*

Paper and pencil for Corners activity. (See sample.)

Name _____ Date _____

Places

1. Where you can relax & feel comfortable

   _____

   _____

2. Where you would vacation if you could

   _____

   _____

3. Where you would move to (OK not to)

   _____

   _____

Favorites

1. Song (currently)

   _____

   _____

2. Thing—what you would grab if your house caught fire

   _____

   _____

3. Outdoor activity

   _____

   _____

People

1. Person who makes you feel safe & comfortable

   _____

   _____

2. Person you admire and respect

   _____

   _____

3. Someone you'd like to know better

   _____

   _____

School

1. Subject you like best

   _____

   _____

2. One thing you'd change about your classroom

   _____

   _____

3. A teacher who has been helpful

   _____

   _____

Session 3: Self-Concept Group

■ *Icebreaker and Review:*

Recall how last week students did an activity that helped them get to know each other better and that this is something that will continue each week. Ask if they know the meaning of the word "positive." Discuss. Choose (or assign) partners and share the following sentences. (It might help to have them written down.)

I feel most positive about myself when:

    1. I'm doing _____ .

    2. I'm with _____ .

    3. I'm at _____ .

After sharing, discuss briefly.

■ *Skill-Building or Awareness Activity:*

FEELING-O Game

Part of a healthy self-concept is understanding one's own feelings; using "feeling" words can help students understand their feelings. This game is played like BINGO. FEELING-O cards and the smaller "word cards" (cards with feeling words on them) are made of laminated tag board. Use the same 15 words and make enough cards for the group, mixing the sequence of words so that no two cards are alike. You will need chips to cover words (pieces of paper will do).

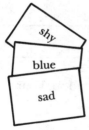

jealous	friendly	angry	shy
surprised	nervous	silly	disappointed
blue	FREE	scared	left-out
excited	sad	cheerful	anxious

sample word cards

Sample FEELING-O card

Since students usually know how to play BINGO, they know what to do. One person has the word cards and calls the words; this person (sometimes the counselor) usually doesn't play. One can win across, down, or diagonally. Winner shouts (softly) "feeling-o." Then group members take turns saying something positive about the winner, or else they use one positive adjective to describe winner. Continue playing until someone who hasn't won wins.

■ *Summary:*

How did it feel to have the group say positive things about you? (Some children will say that it feels uncomfortable—but by the time the group is over this usually changes.) Discuss, if you have time, why some people feel uncomfortable hearing good things about themselves.

■ *Materials:*

FEELING-O cards and word cards; pieces of paper (or some kind of chip—pennies, bottle caps, etc.).

Session 4: Self-Concept Group

(Sessions 4 and 5 are assertiveness training)

■ *Icebreaker:*

Tell children that part of having a positive self-concept is being able to respond assertively to what others say and do. Ask if they have heard this word before. Then discuss concept of "rights." What do they think this means?

■ *Skill-Building or Awareness Activity:*

1. Tell students, "We just talked about 'rights' and 'assertiveness.' If we give up our rights, we teach others to take advantage of us." Discuss times when this may have happened and how it felt.

2. Tell students, "Sometimes people try to stand up for themselves and get into a big fight or argument. Has this ever happened to you? Have you seen it happen to others?" Discuss.

3. Teach three ways of responding to what others say and do.

Response Models:

1. Aggressive—the bully

2. Non-aggressive (or passive)—the doormat

3. Assertive—you stand up for your rights but don't step on rights of others.

    Give sample situation: You brought lunch to school with delicious chocolate cake in it. Friend next to you says, "Oh, can I have that cake, please, please!"

    Have students role-play how a bully and doormat would answer—and how everyone would feel. Teach assertive response: "I know this cake looks good, but I'm hungry, so I think I'll keep it."

4. Teach Kelly-Winship model, as described in Kelly-Winship (1976), as one way of making assertive statements. (This should be on a chart.)

Kelly-Winship model for assertive statements:

1. Let person know you understand how he/she feels.

2. State your problem (how you feel).

3. State what you will do or what you want her/him to do.

    Refer this back to assertive "chocolate cake" answer. Do another example, with students making up the statements.

    Example: Your very favorite TV show is on. Your best friend calls right in the middle of it and wants to tell you about her recent trip to Florida.

Do more examples, eliciting from students the reasons why they might want to make an assertive response to a friend rather than a passive or aggressive one.

■ *Summary:*

After students have had chances to practice responses, ask the following questions: How does it feel to do this? Could you do this? How would you feel if someone responded to you this way?

Tell students that the group will continue with assertiveness training next week. Go around the group and get reactions.

■ *Materials:*

Charts with the three response models written on it and the three-part model for assertive statements.

Session 5: Self-Concept Group

■ *Icebreaker and Review:*

Talk about last week's session. Review (with charts) the three ways to respond to people and the three-part assertive-response model. Go around the group and ask if students practiced this and how it felt. Ask also if it worked. Have them try one more practice example, using their own words, making assertive statements.

■ *Skill-Building or Awareness Activity:*

Tell students that they are going to do some role-playing, some "acting." Divide them into groups of two or three. Have groups separate to practice a role-play to situations that you give them, making up assertive responses in each case. Each group will then have a chance to act out the situation.

Sample role-plays:

1. Your friend asks to borrow paper from you at school. He does this all the time and never pays you back. You are getting tired of this. Today he asks again.

2. You go to McDonald's with a friend and order a milkshake, a cheeseburger, and some fries. You pay, go sit down, and discover that you didn't get the fries.

Children act out role-plays and they are discussed. Everyone may comment and make suggestions. At this point the group is usually comfortable and this is fun.

■ *Summary:*

When role-plays are finished and have been discussed, talk about how it felt to be assertive. (In this kind of group most members are used to being passive rather than aggressive.) Go around the group, filling in this sentence: I (*could-could not*) do this in real life.

Talk about their answers. Have members agree to give it a try!

Session 6: Self-Concept Group

■ *Icebreaker:*

Since this is the last session, discuss what being in the group has been like. ("I think this group has been _____ .") Leader can go first.

■ *Skill-Building or Awareness Activity:*

Tell students, "I think we have all gotten to know each other better, and we have gotten to know ourselves better. I would like now for each of you to design your own personal coat of arms. Do you know what a coat of arms is?" Discuss. "Yours will not be like anyone else's; it will be unique, because you are."

Pass out paper with coat-of-arms outline on it, and crayons or markers. Give directions: coat of arms is divided into six sections.

Section 1: Draw yourself doing something you really enjoy.

Section 2: Draw your favorite place to relax and feel comfortable.

Section 3: Draw yourself doing something that you are really good at doing.

Section 4: Draw some of your favorite people.

Section 5: Draw the way you see yourself as an adult. What might you see yourself doing?

Section 6: Choose three adjectives to describe yourself.

When finished, have students share their coat of arms with the group if they want. With their permission, put coats of arms on your office wall as a memento.

■ *Summary:*

Ask students to complete the following sentences: In this group I learned _____ . I was surprised that _____ .

Ask students if they would like to be in another group. Encourage them at this time to say anything they want to say to each other or to you. After they have had ample time to do this, have them fill out a group evaluation.

Name _____ Date _____

Personal Coat of Arms

1

2

3

4

5

6

Name

Name _____ Date _____

Evaluation Sheet for Group Participants

Please evaluate our group sessions by circling the appropriate answers.

1. Was the time spent in our group sessions worthwhile?   yes   no

2. Did you learn anything about yourself through participation in this group?   yes   no

3. Did you learn anything about getting along with others through participation in this group?   yes   no

4. Given another opportunity, would you choose to participate in another counseling group?   yes   no

5. Were you satisfied with your counselor's leadership in the group sessions?   yes   no

6. Did you ever talk to anyone outside the group about your participation?   yes   no

7. Have you ever discussed our group with your parents?   yes   no

8. Did you look forward to our meeting time?   yes   no

9. Has there been any change in your behavior since participation in our group?   yes   no

■ *Additional Comments*

From *Child Support Through Small Group Counseling* by Lois Landy.

Resources

Kelly, J.D., and B.J. Winship. "A Verbal Response Model of Assertiveness." *Journal of Counseling Psychology*, 1976, 23, 215–220.

Landy, Lois. *Child Support Through Small Group Counseling*. Lois Landy, Savannah, GA 1984.

Celebrating Self

Grade Level: Middle School	
Time Required: Six Sessions	
Authors: Marge Snider, Pat Crate	

This group developed as a result of a grade-level project to identify student self-esteem scores as measured by the Coopersmith Self-Esteem Inventory. Students with a variety of scores were invited to group to celebrate their unique selves and learn about other students.

■ *Group Objectives:*

1. To develop an understanding of the meaning and origin of self-esteem.

2. To identify one's strengths and weaknesses.

3. To participate in activities that emphasize the uniqueness of oneself.

4. To recognize and express one's feelings.

5. To be able to identify two strategies to implement during low-self-esteem periods.

6. To communicate positive perceptions to others.

7. To communicate with others positive perceptions of oneself.

■ *Time:*

Once per week, 45–50 minutes, for 6–8 weeks.

■ *Group Composition:*

Eight to twelve sixth-grade students with varying levels of self-esteem as determined by teachers' recommendations and self-esteem inventory.

■ *Group Rules:*

1. Confidentiality

2. Right to pass

3. One person speaking at a time

4. No put-downs

Session 1: Celebrating Self

■ *Introduction, Housekeeping and Rules:*

1. Collect invitations, take roll, and collect student contracts.

2. Students are welcomed and leaders are introduced. Explain that the purpose of the group is to recognize and explore interests, abilities, strengths, and weaknesses of all group members in a supportive environment. Emphasize that each person is special, unique, and that the group will give each person an opportunity to learn more about himself or herself. It will also give each person a chance to understand, accept, and appreciate other group members.

3. Group rules: Confidentiality; one person talking at a time; no put-downs; right to pass. Ask for additional suggestions from group members. Secure group consensus.

■ *Skill-Building or Awareness Activity:*

"This Is Me" handout. Students break into dyads. Partners interview one another using the sheet, and then partners are introduced to the group. Discussion of similarities and differences.

■ *Summary:*

Ask students what they learned today. Preview second session.

Name _____ Date _____

This Is Me

Name _____

Birthday _____

Favorite TV Show _____

Favorite Movie _____

Favorite Thing to Eat _____

Name Things You Like to Do (hobbies, sports, etc.) _____

_____

This Is Me

Name _____

Birthday _____

Favorite TV Show _____

Favorite Movie _____

Favorite Thing to Eat _____

Name Things You Like to Do (hobbies, sports, etc.) _____

_____

This Is Me

Name _____

Birthday _____

Favorite TV Show _____

Favorite Movie _____

Favorite Thing to Eat _____

Name Things You Like to Do (hobbies, sports, etc.) _____

_____

Session 2: Celebrating Self

■ *Introduction:*

Take roll. Ask a student to volunteer to review group rules.

■ *Icebreaker:*

Ask a volunteer to name group members. Group discussion of similarities and differences learned from last week.

■ *Skill-Building or Awareness Activity:*

1. Thumbprint Activity. Using the theme of uniqueness, the leader uses thumbprints as an example. Each student receives a blank card, puts his or her thumbprint on the front of the card after placing it on an ink pad. He or she puts initials on the back of the card.

   Students break into pairs and compare the similarities and differences of the prints. Students hand in cards. After visualizing their own thumbprint, the cards are passed out and the students try to find their own thumbprint. Discuss uniqueness with the group.

   Alternate activity: Handwriting identification activity, using above procedure. (Each student writes "I am special" on his or her card.)

2. Celebrating Self Game. Explain the game, distribute player sheets. Each student selects a card from the basket, verbalizes his or her answer, and fills in a response on the player card. After a set period of time, the student with the most points is considered the winner for the day. Collect cards to use for next session.

■ *Summary:*

Discuss similarities and differences with the group.

Directions for "Celebrating Self" Game

1. 3 to 6 players may play the game at one time.

2. When it is your turn, select a card and tell the rest of the players about yourself as directed on the card. For example, if you land on *Physical Characteristics*, you must tell the group one of your physical characteristics and write it on your game sheet. Do this for each of the categories.

3. Each category is assigned a different point value. You earn points as the game continues. No more than three items may earn points in any one category. If you draw a card on that category again, you lose your turn.

4. Continue playing for a specified amount of time, then stop and add your scores. The winner is the person with the most points.

5. You may decide to play until a certain number of points is earned. A player cannot earn points unless he or she tells the group members his or her characteristics, friendship qualities, interests, future goals, etc., and writes it on the game sheet.

Note: There should be 3 game cards per category to accommodate a group size of 3–6 players.

"Celebrating Self" Game Cards

Why I Have Friends 15 Points	**Interests** 10 Points
Things I Do Well 20 Points	**Physical Characteristics** 5 Points
Choose Any Category	**Future Goals** 10 Points

Group Counseling for School Counselors

Name _____ Date _____

"Celebrating Self" Game Sheet

Physical Characteristics		Interests	
_____ 5 pts.		_____ 10 pts.	
_____ 5 pts.		_____ 10 pts.	
_____ 5 pts.		_____ 10 pts.	

Future Goals		Why I Have Friends	
_____ 10 pts.		_____ 15 pts.	
_____ 10 pts.		_____ 15 pts.	
_____ 10 pts.		_____ 15 pts.	

Things I Do Well

_____ 20 pts.

_____ 20 pts.

_____ 20 pts.

Total _____

Group Counseling for School Counselors

Session 3: Celebrating Self

■ *Icebreaker:*

Ask group members to tell what they do when they feel low.

■ *Skill-Building or Awareness Activity:*

1. Continue "Celebrating Self" game. At conclusion of the game, each student tells the other group members the accomplishments, strengths, interests, and future goals listed on his or her score card. Before the students read their score cards, the leader discusses the difference between bragging and saying positive things about oneself.

2. "I Feel Really Good About Myself" sheet. Students complete sentence stem. Share with partners or in large group.

■ *Summary:*

Ask students to share something they learned today. Preview Session 4.

I Feel Really Good About Myself

Write a definite, positive experience you have had for each topic.

I feel (or, I felt) really good about myself . . .

1. when with my own hands I made a . . . _____

   _____

2. when my best friend and I . . . _____

   _____

3. when doing the best I could I . . . _____

   _____

4. when I had a fun time at . . . _____

   _____

5. when, even though it was hard, I was honest about . . . _____

   _____

6 when I showed my skill in . . . _____

   _____

7. when with my family I . . . _____

   _____

8. when in school I . . . _____

   _____

9. when a teacher and I . . . _____

   _____

10. when I made others happy . . . _____

    _____

11. when someone I love and I . . . _____

    _____

Session 4: Celebrating Self

■ *Icebreaker:*

Pass around a mirror. Have students complete this sentence: "When I look in the mirror, I feel good about . . . " (my smile, my braces, my eyes, etc.).

■ *Skill-Building or Awareness Activity:*

1. Ask students to write down one thing they are not doing now—either at home, school, or with friends—that would make life easier for them. (For example: do my homework, make my bed, feed my pet, get up on time, fix my hair.) Write it on slip entitled Group Goal Sheet (see page 31) and turn it in. Discuss how they will achieve their goals.

2. Read poem "Self-Esteem":

   Today I don't feel good about me or about you.
   I think I made everything look blue.
   I know there is O.K.ness in all of us here
   But somehow today it just won't shine clear.
   I know I have things that are good about me.
   Today I can't seem to set them free.
   If you were me on this very day
   > How would you help me?
   > What would you say?

■ *Discussion:*

This poem reflects the way a person felt on a particular day. Does that person feel good or bad about himself that day? How many people ever had days when they felt that way? What helps you when you're having a bad day? What things do you do to help you feel better? What keeps you feeling low? *Who* helps you feel better? What kinds of things make you feel bad?

3. Have students write an anonymous letter to Dear Abby about something they have had a hard time dealing with. (Leader could mention a few examples.) Collect letters. They will be discussed at the next group session.

Session 5: Celebrating Self

■ *Icebreaker:*

Ask students to complete the following: One thing I can teach someone else is . . . .

■ *Skill-Building or Awareness Activity:*

1. Students complete goal sheets and discuss them.

2. Discuss Dear Abby letters from last week's session. Use problem-solving techniques when discussing letters.

■ *Summary:*

Remind students that next week will be the last session.

Session 6: Celebrating Self

■ *Icebreaker:*

Sharing Activity. Pass out 3 × 5 card to each student. Let students write their name in middle. In each of four corners, ask them to write following things about themselves:

interests
strengths
accomplishments
something they like about themselves

■ *Skill-Building or Awareness Activity:*

1. Continue discussion of Dear Abby letters.

2. Strength Bombardment Activity: Each student is given a brightly colored piece of paper with a group member's name on it. Each student writes a positive comment about that person on the sheet and continues to write comments and trade sheets with group members until each person's sheet is filled with positive comments. When the activity is completed, each member reads another's sheet to the group and presents the completed sheet to the person to keep.

3. Students complete evaluation forms.

■ *Summary:*

Students are presented with a Group Participation Certificate.

YOU HAVE SUCCESSFULLY
COMPLETED ____ GROUP.
YOU HAVE MADE NEW
FRIENDS, DEVELOPED NEW
IDEAS, LEARNED TO
COMMUNICATE,
AND LISTENED TO OTHERS.

_____
COUNSELOR

YOU HAVE SUCCESSFULLY
COMPLETED ____ GROUP.
YOU HAVE MADE NEW
FRIENDS, DEVELOPED NEW
IDEAS, LEARNED TO
COMMUNICATE,
AND LISTENED TO OTHERS.

_____
COUNSELOR

Refusal Skills

Grade Level: Middle School and High School	
Time Required: Six Sessions	
Author: John Patrick Huerta	

■ *How This Group Developed:*

John first received Refusal Skills training in 1985 from the Prevention Resource Center in Boulder, Colorado. He has been using the model in the classroom and in small groups ever since. The need for a refusal-skills group has evolved from the Reagan Administration's "Just Say No" campaign. While probably very effective for elementary-age students, many middle-school-age students have expressed feelings that "Just Say No" is not enough to resist the internal and external pressures of adolescence.

■ *Group Objective:*

The refusal-skills group is designed to give students a practical model for saying no to negative peer pressure. The 5-step model leads the student through the process of logical decision making, thereby generating positive alternatives to peer pressure. The teaching process involves role-playing and modeling each step of the skill to students, helping them practice, and coaching them throughout the learning experience.

■ *Time:*

45-minute periods, six weekly sessions

■ *Group Composition:*

Refusal Skills has been taught to small groups of 6–10 students and has also been taught to regular classes of 25–30.

■ *Group Rules:*

Standard group rules apply:

1. No put-downs

2. Confidentiality

3. Right to pass

Session 1: Refusal Skills Group

■ *Icebreaker:*

Students will describe a situation where teenagers have a hard time saying no. As this is the first meeting, students should write a situation on a sheet of paper without their name on it. The group leader can then read the situations and lead into discussion.

■ *Skill-Building or Awareness Activity:*

Students should discuss the personal effects that peer pressure has on them. *Inclusion* must be introduced as a basic need of teens, and the power that the need to belong has over their behavior. The goals of Refusal Skills will then be introduced and discussed. The goals of Refusal Skills are:

1. To keep your friends
2. To stay out of trouble
3. To have fun

■ *Summary:*

Is it possible to say no and still meet the three goals of the Refusal Skills model? Solicit from the group any experiences of resisting peer pressure, and discuss whether or not they also achieved the three goals.

Session 2: Refusal Skills Group

■ *Icebreaker:*

Review the name of each group member. If necessary, a group inclusion activity such as a name game should be used to validate each person as a member of the group.

■ *Review:*

Review the three goals of Refusal Skills.

■ *Skill-Building or Awareness Activity:*

Introduce the Refusal Skills model by passing out the first handout and explaining the steps. The five steps are:

1. Ask questions.

2. Name the trouble.

3. Identify the consequence.

4. Suggest an alternative, then start to leave.

5. Keep the door open.

Describe a personal situation to illustrate the 5-step model, reviewing each step and explaining how each step was helpful. Each step of the model assists in decision making and consequently may influence friends positively by giving them more information. Specifically:

1. *Ask Questions.* Determine if it is a situation that will involve trouble. Encourage students not to be afraid to ask "dumb" questions. Too many times we get in trouble or make poor decisions because we don't think—we just do. Step 1 ensures that at least one person in the group will encourage others to think about the situation.

2. *Name the Trouble.* Too many kids base decisions on faulty information, e.g., "It's not burglary if the window is open." (A worksheet is provided for Session 3 primarily to gather information and to discuss what is right and wrong.)

3. *Identify the Consequences.* Decide what you will be risking and express your thoughts. Again, many students do not consider all of the consequences of a decision. Step 3 encourages them to consider not only the legal but also the social, personal, and health consequences of a decision. Many groups may be influenced positively by Step 3, and the student has effectively resisted peer pressure just by getting his or her friends to think.

4. *Suggest an Alternative, Then Start to Leave.* If a person still finds himself being pressured after the first three steps, then he needs to suggest an alternative and leave. This step is the key to saying no and still achieving the three goals. It is very important to teach that one should not engage in an argument or discussion over the merits of the negative or positive alternative. The good guys do not always win these arguments, so don't even start. Suggest something positive and then leave. Many kids are looking for a way out; and while a positive alternative may not sway the whole group, there are many who are looking for something that will not involve trouble. (The worksheet for Session 4 is designed to generate alternatives.)

5. *Keep the Door Open.* Encourage the students not to put down or threaten the group that they are leaving if they want to achieve the three goals. However, many may choose to end a friendship if the stakes are too high.

Choose a low-level peer-pressure situation suggested by the group, and role-play. The group leader should take the role of the "good guy" and the "bad guy" in order to ensure proper modeling at the start of the learning process. In subsequent role-plays, the counselor plays the bad guy and the students play the good guy. The counselor offers corrective feedback (coaching) after each role-play, first asking other group members for their evaluation. After the role-play, discuss whether the five steps were followed and whether or not the "good guy" achieved the three goals.

■ *Summary:*

Recite the 5 steps of the Refusal Skills model.

■ *Materials:*

Refusal Skills handout

Refusal Skills

Steps

1. ***Ask questions***—*"Why . . . where . . .?"* Determine if it is a situation that will involve trouble.

2. ***Name the trouble***—*"That's . . . ."* Tell your friend the real or legal name of the trouble.

3. ***Identify the consequences***—*"If I get caught . . . ."* Tell your friend what you will be risking. Legal, family, school, self-image, job, and health.

4. ***Suggest an alternative, then start to leave***—*"Why don't we . . . ."* Suggest something else that is fun and legal.

5. ***Keep the door open***—*"If you change your mind . . . ."* Leave and invite your friend to join you if he/she decides to come later.

Group Counseling for School Counselors

Sessions 3 & 4: Refusal Skills Group

■ *Icebreaker and Review:*

Recite the 5 steps and ask if anyone has had a chance to use the model.

■ *Skill-Building or Awareness Activity:*

Students will complete the Consequences worksheet (Session 3) or the Alternatives worksheet (Session 4), either individually or in pairs. After completing the worksheet, the group will go over the worksheet to answer any questions and to ensure that everyone has the correct information.

■ *Summary:*

Today I learned . . . or I was surprised that . . . .

■ *Materials:*

Session 3—Consequences Worksheet
Session 4—Alternatives Worksheet

Name _____ Date _____

Consequences—What Might Happen!

For each of the troubles below, list the consequences. Also, fill in the legal name for that trouble, if any.

Trouble	Consequences				
Situation	Legal	School	Family	You	Others
1. Taking a record from a store without paying					
2. Smoking pot					
3. Skipping school					
4. Getting drunk with friends					
5. Cheating on a test					
6. Painting words on a public building					
7.					
8.					

Group Counseling for School Counselors

Name _____ Date _____

Alternatives Worksheet

Place	Your friend wants to . . .	"Instead, why don't we . . . ."	How do you say it and still keep your friends?
Class	1. cheat on a test 2. copy someone's homework 3. pass notes 4.		
Cafeteria	1. have a food fight 2. steal lunch money 3. 4.		
On the weekend	1. sneak out of your house late at night 2. have a party when your parents are out of town 3. go to a keg party 4.		
Parking lot	1. get high 2. steal tapes from some-one's car 3. 4.		
After school	1. smoke cigarettes 2. leave without paying bill at restaurant 3. 4.		
	1. 2. 3.		

Group Counseling for School Counselors

Sessions 5 & 6: Refusal Skills Group

■ *Review:*

By this point we want to avoid any overkill and hope that the students have assimilated the 5 steps to some degree. Point out that we are now ready to apply learning to "real" situations by having students role-play the "good guys" using the five steps.

■ *Skill-Building or Awareness Activity:*

Students volunteer to role-play the "good guys," and the counselor plays the "bad guy" in peer situations that the group has suggested. (The National PTA has been on record as being opposed to students role-playing the "bad guys," since it provides practice in negative behavior. We strongly recommend that you have students role-play only the "good guys" when the role-play involves controversial issues or illegal activities.) It is important to choose relatively easy situations at first to ensure initial student success. Situations that have attractive alternatives are usually the best. If necessary, the group leader can "freeze" the action if a student gets stuck. Freeze the action, solicit help or suggestions from the group, and then continue. The group leader can take the role of a coach on the sideline to assist the "good guy" to effectively resist peer pressure.

■ *Summary:*

Discuss the practicality and relevancy of the Refusal Skills model.

Resources

Colorado Prevention Resource Center
Boulder, Colorado

Quest International
537 Jones Road
Granville, Ohio 43023-0566

Handling Conflict: Stand Up to Bullies

Grade Level: Middle School	
Time Required: Six Sessions	
Author: Sharon Pittman	

■ *How This Group Developed:*

The Stand Up to Bullies group is for middle-school students who are tired of being pushed around by others. The group is designed to teach assertiveness and good communication skills and encourage greater risk-taking. Fifth- and sixth-graders have participated, but the group can be adapted to any grade.

The idea for a Stand Up to Bullies group came from a presentation by Ann Cooper and Linda Worley at the 1985 GSCA Fall Conference.

Session 1: Handling Conflict

■ *Introduction:*

1. Overview of Group

   - Explain time, location, and number of sessions to students.

   - Explain purpose of group. Example: The purpose of this group is to learn and practice new skills to use with bullies.

   - Tell students what it is like to be in a group.

   - Have students make a commitment to risk acting a new way.

2. Leader's Views on Standing Up to Bullies

   - It is possible to handle bullies without getting into a fight. The leader does not advocate fighting.

   - Standing up for yourself without fighting is a skill you can learn.

   - Each person is responsible for his or her own behavior.

   - It's hard to make progress unless you're willing to risk trying something new.

3. Group Structure

   - Do a name-learning activity if group members do not know each other.

   - Have students make rules for the group. Suggestions:

     - Keep what we say in group confidential.

     - Talk to other group members, not just the leader.

     - Listen and support each other.

     - Don't interrupt or put anyone down.

   - Explain role of leader and participants in a group experience.

     - Students have a right to ask questions.

     - Students have a right to pass.

     - Sometimes the leader will talk to the group about what he or she sees happening in the group.

     - Sometimes the leader will point out what one person is doing, and that person may feel that he or she is on the "hot seat."

■ *Icebreaker:*

   - Students are asked to think of a bully they have known.

   - Have the group break into pairs.

   - One person of each pair chooses to be "A," the other person "B."

■ *Icebreaker: (continued)*

- A's talk about their bully for one minute while B's listen. The name of the bully should not be mentioned. Be sure to model appropriate listening skills for students.

- B's talk about their bully while A's listen.

- Process the activity with students.

  - Which role did you find easier? Why?

  - What did your bully and your partner's bully have in common?

■ *Skill-Building or Awareness Activity:*

Characteristics of Bullies

Have students brainstorm characteristics of bullies. Write their list on chart paper and hang it on the wall. Example from one fifth-grade group:

Bullies

- think they can beat everybody up
- talk behind your back
- use you
- are more often boys than girls
- look for a fight
- do mean things

- act like they're better than you
- brag a lot
- don't respect your things
- lie
- pick on you

Characteristics of People Who Get Bullied

Have students brainstorm characteristics of victims of bullies. What do we all have in common when we get bullied? Write this list on chart paper and hang also. Example from same group:

People Who Get Bullied

- are less mean
- want to fight back
- have something about them that invites bullies to pick on them

- are afraid
- are scared to say something back
- sometimes act wimpy

■ *Summary/Homework:*

Have students select something from the People Who Get Bullied list that they would be willing to work on during the week. Example: Figure out what it is about you that invites others to pick on you.

Session 2: Handling Conflict

■ *Icebreaker:*

Review of names.

■ *Review:*

1. Have students complete this sentence: "What I remember from last time is . . . ."
2. Discuss homework.

■ *Skill-Building or Awareness Activity:*

Body Language Lesson

- Pass out handout on body language.

- Explain terms *aggressive*, *assertive*, and *passive*.

- Have students demonstrate each type of body language.

Role-Play Activity

- Have students walk around the room making eye contact with each group member and practicing assertive body language.

- Process the activity. What was that like for you? Where would that be hard to do? Why?

■ *Summary/Homework:*

Ask students what they learned today. Ask them to practice assertive body language this week.

Name _____ Date _____

Body Language

Aggressive

Hands on hips
Loud
Sarcastic
Air of superiority
Narrowed eyes
Stare down
Finger pointing
Clenched fist
Put-downs
Crowding the other person

Passive

Anxious
Pleading
Sing-song voice
Overly soft
Frequent throat clearing
Little eye contact
Laughs and winks
   when expressing anger
Lack of self-confidence
Stepping back from the person
Covering the mouth with hand

Assertive

Good eye contact
Voice appropriately loud and firm
Lean slightly forward
Attitude of respect for self and others

Session 3: Handling Conflict

■ *Icebreaker/Review:*

- "What I remember from last time is . . . ."
- Discuss homework: How did you try to change your body language? What happened?

■ *Skill-Building or Awareness Activity:*

Brainstorm

- What could you say to a bully that would be assertive? What do you think would happen if you tried it? Could it get what you want without changing you into a bully?

Assertiveness Map 1 ("I" Messages)

- Explain how to use Assertiveness Map 1
- Example: *"When you take my things without my permission, I feel angry, because . . . I can't find them when I need them."*
- Have students think up examples where it would be appropriate to use the map.

Dyads

- Role-play, using Assertiveness Map 1 with partner.

■ *Summary/Homework:*

- Use Assertiveness Map 1 on someone this week.
- Continue to practice assertive body language.

Assertiveness Map 1

When you . . .

I feel . . .

because . . .

Assertiveness Map 2

I realize . . .

but . . .

so . . .

Group Counseling for School Counselors

Session 4: Handling Conflicts

■ *Icebreaker/Review:*

- Ask students to complete this sentence: "I used to . . . but now I . . . . "

- Discuss homework: Who used Assertive Map 1? What happened? Do you think you were successful? Why or why not?

■ *Skill-Building or Awareness Activity:*

Assertiveness Map 2

- Explain how to use Assertiveness Map 2.

- Example: *"I realize . . . you don't have enough lunch money, but you haven't paid back the money you borrowed from me last time, so you'll need to borrow from someone else."*

- Have students think up examples where it would be appropriate to use the map.

Dyads

- Role-play, using Assertiveness Map 2 with partner.

■ *Summary/Homework:*

- Use Assertiveness Map 2 on someone this week.

Session 5: Handling Conflict

■ *Icebreaker/Review:*

- Ask students to complete these sentences: "How I've changed since I've been in this group . . . " "What I still need to work on is . . . . "

- Discuss homework: Who used Assertive Map 2? What happened? Do you think you were successful? Why or why not?

■ *Skill-Building or Awareness Activity:*

The Assertion Game

- Go over rules and scoring.

- Use dilemmas from an assertiveness game (such as The Assertion Game* from Childswork/Childsplay) or make up your own situations requiring assertive responses. Chips and spinner can come from any game.

- Have students play the game as a round. Group members must reach consensus on the scoring after hearing one player's response. Body language is part of the score also.

Discuss the Game

- Are you happy with your score? How could you have made your score higher?

■ *Summary/Homework:*

- Students design their own homework for the last week.

---

*The Assertion Game is for children who have experienced violation of their rights. Cost is $49.50 from Childswork/Childsplay, Center for Applied Psychology—3rd Floor, 441 N. 5th St., Philadelphia, PA 19123. Phone 1-800-962-1141 for catalog. *Assert with Love*, $23.95, from the same company, is also good.

Session 6: Handling Conflict

■ *Icebreaker/Review:*

- What did you choose for homework? Why?

- How did it go?

- What do you still need to work on?

■ *Skill-Building or Awareness Activity:*

Process the Group Experience

- How was it different from what you expected?

- How have you changed since you've been in group?

Evaluation of the Group

- Have students silently complete a Group Evalution Sheet.

- Allow students to share answers if they want to.

- On the back of the evaluation sheet, have students pay themselves for being a group member. Students write down a dollar amount they feel they earned for their performance as a group member. Students pay themselves between $.01 and $10.00. This is a good time to go over the group rules again and the purpose of the group.

■ *Summary/Closure:*

- Point out progress and success to individual group members.

- Invite students to point out each other's progress and success.

- Process the group experience so everyone understands what happened in the group.

- Share what you liked about these group members.

- Allow time to chat informally and celebrate the end of group.

SPECIAL-CONCERN GROUPS

- Family
- Loss
- At Risk
- Buddy System
- Pregnancy
- New Student

Family Group (Divorce)

Grade Level: Upper Elementary, Middle School, and High School	
Time Required: Ten Sessions	
Author: Barbara Earley	

■ *Purpose:*

Family group offers students the opportunity to meet with others who share similar experiences. Students who join the family group have parents who are separated, divorced, or remarried. Often students feel that their situation is unique, that no one else has felt the way they do. The group provides opportunities for self-awareness, sharing with others, problem-solving, and better communication skills within their families.

■ *Composition:*

The 6–10 students can come from a combination of grade levels. They can be in various stages, from those who experienced divorce five years ago as well as those currently involved in divorce. It is advised, however, not to have students in the group who are still in shock over a separation and are not yet ready for a group experience. Students who were involved in divorce years ago can be role models to help students realize that there are other stages besides the immediate crisis stage. Since students are sometimes reluctant to join this type of group it is helpful to meet with them individually a week or so before group begins.

■ *Length of Time:*

Groups meet once per week for 10 weeks. For those who need additional support, you may provide a support group once a month for the rest of the year, as well as individual counseling.

Advice to the Group Leader

1. Get parent permission for the child to be in group.

2. Be careful to not let your value judgments show. It is sometimes difficult to remain impartial.

3. Help students understand that they are not responsible for the divorce. Sometimes parents, in their anger and frustration, tell children they are the reason.

4. Allow students to express their emotions.

5. Teach them skills—communication, assertiveness—to keep them out of the middle. Children frequently complain that each parent talks about the other and questions them about the other parent's activities.

6. Get one or both parents involved if you think it would benefit the child. Sometimes parents are unaware of the consequences of their actions. You may also want to refer the parent to outside counseling, groups, or related reading materials.

7. Let the teachers know—but without a lot of details—if you think the child's grades are being affected by the divorce.

Session 1: Family Group

■ *Introduction:*

The counselor may want to begin this way:

"Some of you may have parents who have recently separated, are divorced, or who have divorced and remarried, giving you additional parents and families. Students have found this group to be very helpful because they can share their feelings with other students who have similar experiences. You may remember times when you felt alone and thought no one else could possibly understand what you were feeling. Or you may have felt embarrassed, ashamed, guilty, angry, or hurt. These feelings are all normal, and represent the different stages we go through when we have a break-up in our family.

"At the end of these ten weeks, I hope you will have learned some new skills to help you adjust to your situation, to understand what has happened, and to improve the communication within your family."

■ *Icebreaker:*

Ask the students to tell their name, grade, and a brief summary of their family situation (how long their parents have been divorced or separated, whom they are living with, and what their biggest family concerns are at this time). Give them 30 seconds to think about what they want to say. The counselor may introduce himself/ herself first to get the group started.

After the introductions, ask the following questions:

1. What are some things you noticed we had in common with each other?

2. Sometimes it's helpful to remember that others have problems similar to ours. How many of you have ever felt that you were the only one who had divorced parents, or felt that no one else understood?

■ *Rules and Housekeeping:*

Let students come up with the rules, but be sure they include:

1. What is said in group is confidential.
2. Don't put each other down.

    Parent letter is given out and explained. Remind students that the group meets once per week for 10 weeks. They are expected to make up the work they miss while in the group. (You may want to go around and ask each person what class is being missed and how the work will be made up.)

    Address any comments or questions.

Session 1: Family Group *(continued)*

■ *Skill-Building or Awareness Activity:*

Ask students to think about this sentence: "One thing that has improved since the divorce/separation is . . . ." Give them a minute, then go around the circle and ask students to respond.

■ *Summary:*

Remind students to return the letter in order to attend group next time.

Remind students that you are available to them on an individual basis as well as in the group.

Dear Parents,

We would like to acquaint you with the counseling services at our school. In addition to individual counseling, classroom guidance, and parent-teacher conferences, we offer group sessions that deal with specific concerns. Topics such as getting along with others, making friends, decision making, communicating in the family, handling peer pressure, and nutrition are offered to students.

We have invited your student to join one of our groups that emphasizes communicating in the family. Many students think of themselves as having problems that no one else has. In the group they discover that other students have the same kinds of problems. For students who have been through a divorce, a separation, or a remarriage, it is frequently a comfort to learn how to accept the situation, build better communication in the family, and then go on with life.

Your son/daughter has expressed an interest in this group. If you would like to know more about the group, please call. Also, please sign and return this letter to our office.

Sincerely yours,

_____

Parent Signature

Session 2: Family Group

■ *Icebreaker:*

Greet the group and collect the parent letters. Ask students to complete this sentence: My name is . . . and today I'm feeling . . . (on a 1 to 10 scale—1 is the pits and 10 is the top of the world). After everyone has responded, ask who can name everyone in the group.

■ *Skill-Building or Awareness Activity:*

1. Introduce filmstrip: *My Parents Are Getting a Divorce* (Part 1). Ask students to write down any ideas that occur to them during the filmstrip—something they agree or disagree with, or something they haven't thought of before. Ask them about those ideas when the filmstrip is over.

2. Discuss ideas from filmstrip: What was similar to your situation? What was different?

3. Bibliography. Show students library books on divorce. Encourage them to read one during the next 10 weeks. (See bibliography at the end of Session 10. You may wish to collect magazine articles on divorce. Ask your media specialist for the BookFinder, a book that lists children's books by special topics.)

■ *Summary:*

Today I learned . . . .
Today I relearned . . . .
Today I was surprised that . . . .

Session 3: Family Group

■ *Icebreaker:*

I wish my mother would . . . .
I wish my dad would . . . .
This week has been . . . .

■ *Skill-Building or Awareness Activity:*

1. Filmstrip: *My Parents Are Getting a Divorce* (Part 2). (There are many other videos and filmstrips available on the topic of divorce.) Ask students to write down three ideas or thoughts that they think are important while watching the filmstrip.

2. After the filmstrip, ask students to discuss similarities and differences related to their own situations. This is a good time to increase students' understanding of their parents' problems and feelings, because often they are only able to focus on how they are feeling.

3. Discuss some positive ways that families can help each other in adjusting to the divorce, separation, or remarriage.

4. Discuss books the students have been reading.

■ *Summary:*

Today I learned . . . .

Session 4: Family Group

■ *Icebreaker:*

What are three things that you will do as a parent if you have children one day? They can be things that your parents do that you like, or things you wish they would do. Write them down. Give students time, then discuss responses.

What's going on at home this week?

Give them time to discuss their weekend visitation with a parent or problems at home.

■ *Skill-Building or Awareness Activity:*

True-False Questionnaire: Ask students to fill out questionnaire. Discuss each item, using your group-leadership skills. Remember to be non-judgmental! Indicate that there are no right or wrong answers.

You may want to discuss their future relationships and how their marriages would not necessarily end in divorce. Sometimes students have already decided that they won't get married. It would be a good time to discuss what kinds of things make a good marriage. (*Traits of a Healthy Family*—see bibliography at end of Session 10—is an excellent book for the purposes of this discussion.)

■ *Summary:*

Today I learned . . . .

True-False Questionnaire

Indicate either T for true or F for false.

1. _____ Parents who don't love each other should stay together for the sake of the children.

2. _____ Parents should tell their children why they are getting a divorce.

3. _____ If your parents are divorced, it is likely that when you grow up you will get a divorce.

4. _____ The parent that you visit should not have rules or make you do work.

5. _____ One parent should not make negative comments about the other parent.

6. _____ Your step-parent has no right to discipline you.

7. _____ Children should be included in the decision of whom the parent remarries.

8. _____ Children should not let their parents know how they feel about the divorce.

9. _____ A child should try to make up for the parent who has left by taking on extra responsibilities and being an emotional support to the parent he or she is living with.

10. _____ Children should be able to decide which parent they want to live with.

Session 5: Family Group

■ *Icebreaker:*

Ask students to complete one of the following sentences:
I feel lonely when . . . .
I am happy when . . . .
I wish . . . .

■ *Review:*

Ask students to review the previous session.

■ *Skill-Building or Awareness Activity:*

1. Sentence-Completion Sheet. Students fill out sheet and discuss their answers.

2. Further discussion: What's going on at home?

3. Readings. Discuss books that the students have been reading on the topic of divorce.

4. Have students write anonymous Dear Abby letters, to be turned in to you and discussed the following week. The letters should be written about a current problem that the student is experiencing because of the family situation. They can make up names to sign the letters (like "Worried and Confused") so that when they're read aloud the letters will be anonymous.

■ *Summary:*

I learned . . . .

Sentence Completion

1. When I first found out that my parents were getting a divorce, I felt _____
   _____ .

2. Something I still don't understand about the divorce is _____
   _____ .

3. One thing that I miss is _____
   _____ .

4. A way that I have changed is _____
   _____ .

5. I appreciate my Mom for _____

   but I wish she would _____
   _____ .

6. I appreciate my Dad for _____

   but I wish he would _____
   _____ .

7. When my friends learn that my parents are divorced, they _____
   _____ .

8. The way I feel about divorce is _____
   _____ .

9. I can help other students whose parents are divorced by _____
   _____ .

10. If I could change one thing about myself now, it would be _____
    _____ .

11. Negative effects of the divorce are _____
    _____ .

12. Positive things that have happened because of the divorce are _____
    _____ .

13. Marriage is _____
    _____ .

Session 6: Family Group

■ *Icebreaker:*

One strength I have . . . .

■ *Review:*

Ask students to state one thing they learned in last week's session.

■ *Skill-Building or Awareness Activity:*

Read Dear Abby letters and discuss solutions to problems. The students give advice to each other about what to do in each situation. Then students get into dyads and role-play the situations.

■ *Summary:*

Today I learned . . . .

Session 7: Family Group

■ *Icebreaker:*

Non-listening Exercise

Have students get into pairs. One student talks for one minute about any topic—favorite movies, pet, hobby, or vacation spot. The other student demonstrates not paying attention, interrupting, and any other non-listening practices. Switch roles, but this time have the other person demonstrate what he considers to be good listening practices. Have the group discuss the behaviors that they noticed with not listening and listening. Have a recorder write down the group's lists of behaviors for both.

■ *Skill-Building or Awareness Activity:*

Body Language in Communication

The communication process is always non-verbal as well as verbal. Behavior expresses meaning, sometimes more clearly than words. To be an effective communicator, one must tune in to body language and tone of voice. Consider the following:

70% of what we communicate is through body language.
23% of what we communicate is through tone of voice.
7% of what we communicate is through words.

How we say something is frequently more important than *what* we say.

Explain the importance of non-verbal communication by using the information below. As you go over each item, ask group to demonstrate do's and don'ts.

	Do's	Don'ts
Eyes	good eye contact	stare, glare, jittery, no eye contact
Voice (volume)	loud enough to be heard clearly	too soft or too loud
Voice (tone)	tone communicates understanding	disinterested, gruff tone, sarcastic
Facial expressions	matches your own or other's feeling; smile	frown, yawn, sigh, scowl, blank look
Posture	leaning forward slightly, relaxed	leaning away, rigid, slouching, crossing arms
Movement	toward	away
Distance	arm's length	too close (less than 2 feet); too far (more than 5 feet)

■ *Summary:*

Ask students to summarize the session. Leader should fill in any gaps in their summary. Leader gives overview of next session on communication.

Session 8: Family Group

■ *Icebreaker:*

Ask students to rate how they are feeling, on a scale of 1–10. Ask them to share something positive that's happened to them this past week.

■ *Review:*

Ask students if, during the last week, they paid attention to body language. What did they notice?

■ *Skill-Building or Awareness Activity:*
Communication Skills

1. To introduce communication skills, have the group members respond to the following sentence stems, either orally or in written form.

   I can tell if Mom/Dad is really listening to me when _____

   _____ .

   When I have something bothering me, I let them know by _____

   _____

   _____ .

   When they start giving advice, I feel _____

   _____ .

   I am willing to listen to them if _____

   _____ .

   The best time to talk to Mom/Dad is _____

   _____ .

   When the parent I am visiting makes negative comments about my other parent,
   I _____

   _____ .

2. Discuss with students *appropriate times* to talk with parents or teachers. Talk about being aware of adult moods, and how to best introduce a topic. Suggest that they make an appointment with the parent. Example: "Mom, after we've finished with the dishes tonight, there's some stuff going on at school that I would like to talk with you about. Would you have some time around 8:00?" Students may role-play situations.

■ *Summary:*

Today I learned . . . .

One thing I need to do when communicating with my parents is . . . .

Preview next week's session.

Session 9: Family Group

■ *Icebreaker:*

A time someone listened to me this week was _____ ,

and I could tell they were listening because _____ .

■ *Review:*

Ask students to give examples of communication skills—body language, listening, and timing.

■ *Skill-Building or Awareness Activity:*

I-Message Model

1. When your goals, rights, or safety is being interfered with, *I-messages* are the most appropriate way to communicate what the conflict is to the other person.

    I-messages show your concern in a calm and respectful way.

    We commonly use *you-messages* instead, which accuse and blame the other person and are usually said with anger or sarcasm.

    Listed below are the messages we send with I-messages and you-messages.

I-Messages	*You-Messages*
● I respect you.	● do not show respect
● This is how I feel.	● blame, cause hurt, anger
● This is what I want to happen.	● accuse, ridicule, criticize

    A typical I-message has three parts, which can come in any order.

    I feel *(state feeling)* **when you** *(describe specific behavior)* **because** *(state how it affects you).*

■ *Examples of I-Messages and You-Messages*

a. **I feel** angry **when you** tell something I told you in secret **because** I didn't want anyone else to know.

(You-message: You can't ever keep a secret. I'm never going to speak to you again.)

b. **I feel** irritated **when you** back out of going at the last minute **because** it leaves me stuck with no one to go with.

(You-message: You're always messing up my plans. I can never count on you.)

c. **I feel** upset **when you** tell me to tell Dad stuff about the child support **because** it makes him mad and messes up my weekend.

Session 9: Family Group *(continued)*

(You-message: You're ruining my weekends because you're too weak to talk to Dad yourself.)

d. **I feel** lonely **when you** are gone all the time **because** I miss us doing things together.

(You-message: You're always leaving me here alone. You're so selfish.)

2. Take a situation from the previous Dear Abby letters, and have students role-play, using the I-message model.

3. Have students describe briefly on paper a problem they are having with a parent right now. Allow 3–4 minutes. In dyads, students take turns being the person who has the problem and give an I-message to the other person. The person receiving the message checks the accuracy of the I-message against the following checklist.

I-Messages Checklist

A. Did you:

Say in one brief sentence what you were mad about, by
—describing the specific behavior that was upsetting;
—telling the person how you felt about the behavior;
—stating how the behavior affected you.

B. Were you careful not to:

—blame, put down, or criticize;
—bring up the past, threaten, or accuse;
—get caught up in winning rather than solving the conflict?

4. If there is time, some participants may role-play their situations in front of the group.

5. Assignment: Find a time this week to use an I-message with your parent.

■ *Summary:*

Today I learned . . .

Session 10: Family Group

■ *Icebreaker:*

One way I have grown since this divorce is . . . .

■ *Review:*

Have students review the topics discussed in the divorce group and how these issues have affected their lives. Allow time for students to fill out evaluations and then have discussion.

■ *Summary:*

What I have learned from this group . . . .

■ *Closure:*

Leader wrap-up includes discussion of seeking outside help, having someone to talk to, and problems that parents may be having. Encourage students to come to you individually. You may wish to continue with a once-a-month support group during the year.

Name _____ Date _____

Divorce Group Evaluation

1. The first time that this group met, I felt _____
   _____ .

2. I learned _____
   _____ .

3. The most helpful part of this group _____
   _____ .

4. Something I would change _____
   _____ .

5. I wish _____
   _____ .

6. It would have been more helpful if _____
   _____ .

7. When I told my parents about this group _____
   _____ .

8. Would you recommend this group to your friends? _____

9. Comments: _____
   _____ .

                   Group Counseling for School Counselors

Suggestions from Middle-School Students in Family Group

- Don't have arguments with your ex and then take it out on your kid.

- Do more things with me.

- Spend time with me.

- When you get remarried don't forget I'm still here.

- Don't put bad ideas into my head about my dad/mom.

- Don't put me in the middle.

- Don't tell me things that you don't want my mom/dad to know.

- Don't leave me alone.

- Don't play favorites.

- Don't influence my decision about whom to live with.

- Don't put me on a guilt trip: "If you leave you can't come back!"

Resources for Divorce Groups

Blue, Rose. *A Month of Sundays.* Watts, New York, 1972.

Blume, Judy. *It's Not the End of the World.* Bradbury Press, New York, 1972.

Bowden, Nina. *The Runaway Summer.* Lippincott, Philadelphia, 1969.

Brown, Lauren and Mark. *The Dinosaur's Divorce.* Paperbacks for Educators, Washington, Missouri, 1986.

Gardner, Richard A. *The Boys and Girls Book about Divorce.* Paperbacks for Educators, Washington, Missouri, 1971.

Holland, Isabelle. *Heads You Win, Tails I Lose.* Lippincott, Philadelphia, 1973.

Klein, Norma. *It's Not What You Expect.* Pantheon, New York, 1973.

Mann, Peggy. *My Dad Lives in a Downtown Motel.* Doubleday, New York, 1973.

Reynolds, Marjorie. *The Cabin on Ghostly Pond.* Harper & Row, New York, 1962.

Stolz, Mary. *Leap Before You Look.* Harper & Row, New York, 1972.

Kalb, Jonah, and David Viscott, M.D. *What Every Kid Should Know.* Houghton Mifflin, Boston, 1976.

■ *Filmstrips*

Getting Used to Divorce. EEM Personal Enrichment Series, Grade 5–9, Random House, 1-800-638-6460.

My Parents Are Getting a Divorce. Human Relations Media, 343 Manville Road, Pleasantville, New York 10570.

Loss Group

Grade Level: All Levels	
Time Required: Six Sessions	
Authors: Greg Brigman, Barbara Earley	

A loss group provides a support system for students who have experienced the death of a parent or other family member. These students may have difficulty accepting the death and expressing their feelings. They often act brave and believe the feelings will go away. They think no one understands. Frequently there are unresolved conflicts, feelings of abandonment, anger, and guilt. They may be in a stage of limbo, not able to move ahead because they feel as if their life is over.

Before the group begins, talk with each child in an individual session to let him or her know what the group is about and to learn what his or her particular situation is.

It is important that you feel comfortable with the topic of death before leading a group. There are many good books and journal articles on helping kids deal with loss. Since this topic involves deep feelings, we could not encourage anyone to attempt this group without doing background reading and having some experience leading other types of groups.

Know your own feelings about death. Tune in to your philosophy and beliefs, but be careful about discussing your religious beliefs with students. Look at the losses in your life and how you have dealt with them. Some introspection is helpful before you start writing lesson plans. During the group, maintain an attitude of acceptance, concern, and caring.

Session 1: Loss Group

■ *Introduction:*

Introduce yourself and explain the purpose of the group:

"This is a loss group, and I know that you have experienced a loss in your family. We'll be meeting each week at this time to share with each other how things are going and how you are feeling. This group will be a place where you can talk openly about how you are feeling.

"Sometimes your friends may not understand what you are going through and you may not have anyone to talk to. I have found in leading groups like this that students feel more comfortable talking about death when they realize others have had similar experiences."

■ *Icebreaker:*

"I'd like for us to begin by going around the group, stating your name and what your particular situation is. Tell us who has died in your family, when it happened, and any details you would like to share with the group."

Talking about their situation in front of the group could emit deep feelings and emotions. Be prepared to use your reflective-listening and group-leadership skills.

■ *Skill-Building or Awareness Activity:*

1. Discuss with students how friends sometimes don't know what to say. "What are some of the responses you have received when your friends found out about the death?" (Students report that friends sometimes don't say anything, make inappropriate remarks, or ask questions about specific details of the death.)

   "Adults often offer platitudes: 'He's better off because he doesn't have to suffer,' or 'It was his time to go.' None of these exchanges helps us in our grief. Our friends want to help; but because they feel awkward and uncomfortable, they may say the wrong things. What would you like for your friends to say? What would be helpful? If someone you knew were to experience a death of someone close to him or her, what would you do or say?"

2. Show students some books on death from the school library. Briefly explain each one, and let them check out the books to take home.

   You may read some passages aloud to the group. *Learning to Say Good-Bye* by Eda Le Shan is a helpful book to read to upper-elementary-, middle-, or high-school students.

■ *Summary:*

Today I learned . . . .
I relearned . . . .
I was surprised that . . . .

Session 2: Loss Group

■ *Icebreaker:*

My name is . . . and I wish . . . .

■ *Skill-Building or Awareness Activity:*

1. Begin discussion with the following: "In our lives we experience many kinds of losses, not just death. What are some other losses you have had?"

    Students will mention loss of friendships, moving, losing a favorite posses-sion, losing a favorite teacher, having something stolen from them, or losing a pet. Allow students to discuss their particular situations and how they felt when it happened. "What were the feelings you experienced in the beginning, a little later, and when did you finally accept what happened?"

2. Let students know that people experience any kind of loss in stages. According to Dr. Kubler-Ross, in her book *On Death and Dying*, the stages of grief are:

    denial — *not me — it can't be true*   *Sadness*
    anger — *why me, it's not fair*   *Anger*
    bargaining — *yes me — but if only, or I'd give up to have them back!*   *Guilt*
    depression — *yes me, poor me*   *Relief*
    acceptance — *yes me, but I can learn to deal with the loss*   *Fear*
                                                                            anxiety

    List these stages on a chart and have the group members personalize their situa-tion and discuss how they went through the various stages, and in what order. A person in grief can move back and forth between stages, or can remain stuck in a stage before finally reaching the acceptance stage.

    Ask each student: Which stage are you in now?

    For those students who may not be in the acceptance stage, use your best empathy and caring skills to help them explore their feelings. Your goal is not to move them to the acceptance stage, but to allow them to state their feelings while you listen and remain there for them.

■ *Summary:*

I learned . . . .
I can see that I need to . . . .

www. elisabethkublerross. com
www .bereavement.org /e_ kubler-ross. htm

Session 3: Loss Group

■ *Icebreaker:*

My name is . . . and today I feel . . . .

■ *Review:*

Ask students to remember the five stages of grief.

■ *Skill-Building or Awareness Activity:*

"Today I would like to give each of you some time to share with us what is going on with you. As I talk with each person, the rest of you think about how your feelings and experiences are similar or different. Here are some questions I would like for you to think about:

Since the loss occurred in your family, how has your life changed?

What is difficult for you right now?

What needs working on or needs to be improved?

"Let me give you a minute to think about those questions and we'll begin when you're ready." Give thinking time. "Would someone volunteer to begin our discussion? Maria, you look like you're ready to begin. How has your life changed?"

Gently move through the questions, allowing enough time so every group member will have a chance to participate before the period is over.

Leave some time at the end of the session to show similar experiences of group members. Pull together the idea that everyone has situations that need to be improved, and perhaps some of these situations are normal in any family, not just grieving families.

■ *Summary:*

I learned . . . .
I relearned . . . .
I see that I need to . . . .

Session 4: Loss Group

■ *Icebreaker:*

The high point of my week was when . . . .

■ *Review:*

Spend time summarizing similar experiences that the group shared from last week's activity.

■ *Skill-Building or Awareness Activity:*

1. "Focus on a happy memory that you have of the person you have lost. Perhaps there was a vacation you shared, a funny experience, or an especially happy event. I'll give you some thinking time, and then we'll go around the circle and let each person share a happy memory." Have each group member share his or her happy memory. Process the activity by pointing out similarities, differences, and giving affirmation for sharing their personal experiences.

2. "If you could write a letter to that person right now, what would you like to say? Would you like to tell the person how you are doing, about a happy memory, or what you would like him/her to know?

   "What qualities did that person have that you want to have in your life? What messages about living did he or she give you, either with words or by how he/she lived?

   "I'll give you some paper and time to think. When you're ready, begin your letter with 'Dear . . .' and write whatever you're feeling. This letter is private, so you won't have to share it with group unless you feel like it."

   Allow time for everyone to finish the letter. Allow them to discuss the feelings they had while writing the letter. Permit those students who want to read their letter to the group to do so.

   Sharing these memories often elicits tears and sadness. Sometimes students tune in to the loss of future happy times together. It's important for the counselor not to shut off the expression of sadness. This expression is one key to the healing process. Most people in the student's life are probably uncomfortable with these feelings and don't allow their expression.

■ *Summary:*

I learned . . . .
I relearned . . . .

Session 5: Loss Group

■ *Icebreaker:*

I feel happy when . . . .

■ *Review:*

Allow time for students to express how they felt during last week's activity.

■ *Skill-Building or Awareness Activity:*

1. Show a filmstrip on the topic of death. One that we use is *Spring without Dad.*

2. Have group members list three ideas they got from the filmstrip. Go around the group and have each student share his or her ideas and how they are related to his or her situation.

3. Discuss any books on death the students have read while participating in the group. Encourage them to share their readings and the group discussions with siblings and family members.

■ *Summary:*

I learned . . . .

Session 6: Loss Group

■ *Icebreaker:*

I hope . . . .

■ *Skill-Building or Awareness Activity:*

1. Losses and changes can create stress. Discuss with the group ways to handle stress. Encourage members to get involved in physical activities to alleviate stress.

2. You may want to look at the Children's Stress Scale, an adaptation of the Holmes Stress Inventory, which is found in David Elkind's book, *The Hurried Child.* Be careful in administering the survey to students. You don't want to cause alarm if a student scores high on the number of losses experienced in the past year. Rather, focus on positive activities—hobbies, physical exercise. Use the scale as an awareness technique, pointing out the importance of taking care of yourself to prevent stressful situations. After the group is over, plan to see each group member individually in the next few weeks.

3. If some group members are in need of additional resources, offer to see them individually, have a conference with a family member, or talk to them about counseling from a private therapist or community agency.

   Some students remain in the shock stage for months. Often teachers expect these students to be back to normal after several weeks. It may take a year or longer for students to move to acceptance. The most important part of the healing process is to allow the person to express sadness. If he or she cannot express sadness, long-term problems often result.

4. Written evaluation (see p. 32, Group Evaluation Form).

■ *Summary:*

Something I learned from being in this group is . . . .

Dear Parent:

Your child has chosen to participate in a group to consider loss. Statistics show that one of every twenty children loses a parent during childhood. Very few are prepared to cope with this experience.

This is an important and personal issue and I hope that our discussions in school will be only the beginning of family discussions in the home. It is for this reason that I am notifying you and urging you to contact me at any time you wish. If you have any questions, or anything you would like to share with me concerning your child or the program in general, please call me at xxx-xxxx.

Counselor

_____

Student's Signature

_____

Parent's Signature

Resources for Loss Groups

Bernstein, Joanne. *Loss and How to Cope with It.* Seabury Press, New York, 1977.

Grollman, Earl A. *Explaining Death to Children.* Beacon Press, Boston, 1967.

Hannaford, Mary Joe. *The Joy of Sorrow.* Petit Publishers, 1983, 1940 Trumbull Dr., Dunwoody, GA 30338.

Kubler-Ross, Elisabeth. *On Death and Dying.* Macmillan, New York, 1969.

Le Shan, Eda. *Learning to Say Good-Bye.* Macmillan Publishing Co., New York, 1976.

Le Shan, Eda. *What Makes Me Feel This Way?* Macmillan Publishing Co., New York, 1972.

Le Shan, Eda. *When a Parent is Very Sick.* Joystreet Books, Boston, 1986.

McWilliams, Peter. *How to Survive the Loss of a Love.* Bantam Books, New York, New York, 1984.

Smith, Doris. *A Taste of Blackberries.* T.Y. Crowell, New York, 1973.

Spring without Dad: Coping with Death. EEM Personal Enrichment Series, Grades 5–9. Random House (1-800-638-6460).

At-Risk Group

Grade Level:	Middle School and High School
Time Required:	Ten Sessions
Authors:	Barbara Earley, Marge Snider, Greg Brigman

Every school has a category of students who repeatedly have not been reached by the system. These students may exhibit any or all of the following characteristics and behaviors: apathy, discouragement, disruptive behavior, slow learning, attendance problems, home problems, low self-concept, or performance below ability. These students are not successful.

In the fall of 1987 a committee at our school devised a plan to identify these students. Teachers were asked to list the students who earned five or fewer points and had at least one "U" in an academic subject for each six-week reporting period. At the end of the first two six-week reporting periods, 63 students in grades 6, 7, and 8 were identified. After the next two six weeks, 45 were identified.

The counselors held team meetings in all grade levels to discuss students' performance, standardized test scores, previous grades, attitude, self-concept, attendance, parent contact, counselor intervention, classroom modification, and whether an SST (Student Study Team) referral was appropriate or already in process. After subtracting students who had moved or were in Special Education, 47 students were invited and then scheduled to participate in small-group experiences for a period of eight weeks. The program was voluntary. Parents were notified by letter that their child was not experiencing success and could be in danger of retention. It was suggested that they schedule teacher or counselor conferences, talk with their child in an encouraging manner, and review a list of ideas they were asked to try.

In addition to the group experience, we frequently had parent-teacher conferences, telephone contact, and conferences with students individually. The administration supported the program by attending some of the sessions, talking with the students, and making considerations when students were referred for discipline.

Overall, students in the At-Risk program rated the group experience as positive. They asked for additional meeting times and continued support. Report cards the following year show marked improvement.

Since we began at-risk groups several years ago, we have made some changes. Our groups are now 10 weeks in length, with several monthly follow-up sessions after the regular group ends. It is important that students have contact with the counselor on a regular basis after the group is completed. It is advisable to call the group together once a month or every six weeks during the year to check on their progress and keep them motivated.

Another change is to call the group STAR (Students Taking Academic Responsibility). We recommend a title that sounds more positive than the term "at-risk."

A new aspect of this program is to identify at-risk students at the end of the fifth grade before they come to middle school. In the fall of sixth grade these students will take a six-week study-skills course and be offered Opportunity Group for the second six weeks. Opportunity Group offers small-group tutoring by a paraprofessional. It meets daily during a non-academic period.

A review of the research literature involving school counselor interventions with low-achieving and underachieving elementary-, middle-, and high-school students by Wilson (1982) included the following:

1. Group counseling seems to be more effective than individual counseling.

2. Structured group programs were more effective than unstructured programs.

3. Group programs lasting 8 weeks or less had positive results in only 1 of 5 programs evaluated. Of 9 programs lasting between 9 and 12 weeks, 5 were effective; however, 6 of 8 interventions lasting more than 12 weeks were successful.

4. Programs in which children volunteered for treatment were more successful than programs with nonvoluntary participants.

5. Programs that combined counseling and study skills were most effective.

Session 1: At-Risk Group

■ *Introduction:*

1. Counselor, administrator introduce themselves. Students introduce themselves. Counselor explains the criterion for students to be included in the group: two report cards that show low grades. Ask students:

   - How many think you will do better this time on your report card?

   - How many think you will do about the same?

   - How many think you may have even lower cards than last time?

2. Explain group purpose to students. Example: We wanted to meet with you because we are concerned about your grades and we know you are, too. In fact, if your grades continue as they are now, you are in danger of being retained in the same grade for next year.

   How many of you have thought of that already, or have had a teacher or your parents tell you that?

   How many of you would like to prevent that from happening? We have a plan. For the next 10 weeks we are offering a group that will include activities on:

   > goal setting
   > study-skill tips
   > communicating with your teacher
   > organization
   > motivation

   We will also be sending a letter to your parents explaining the group and asking them to encourage your efforts to improve.

3. Group Rules

   Ask students to suggest rules for the group to work together well. Get consensus on any that you adopt. Ask a student to write these down. Make sure you include the following:

   > no put-downs
   > right to pass
   > confidentiality

■ *Skill-Building or Awareness Activity:*

Hand out Student Self-Evaluation Form. Ask students to rate each of the seven statements from 1–4. Go through each statement, asking for ratings from each student. This usually generates discussion. The leader will need to keep focus on accepting responsibility instead of blaming teacher or others. Let the students know that the group meetings will address areas they feel need improvement.

■ *Summary:*

Ask students to summarize purpose of group; preview some of the areas of focus in the coming meetings.

Student Self-Evaluation Form

Rate yourself 1–4 on each bulleted item below. Follow the rating system listed here.

    1. outstanding   2. above average   3. satisfactory   4. needs improvement

- I participate in class discussion.

- I listen carefully.

- I complete work assigned on time.

- I ask questions when I'm unsure or don't know.

- My conduct is satisfactory.

- I take clear notes on important topics.

- I read all assignments and understand what I read.

Student Letter

Dear

Your report-card grades for the last two six-week periods show that you are not doing well in school. Should these grades continue, you will be in danger of being retained in the same grade next year.

In order to discuss this matter with you, please come to room _____ on _____ at _____ .

Present this letter to your exploratory teacher on that day so you will be excused from class. Bring this letter to the meeting.

Sincerely yours,

Counselors

Parent Letter

Parents of _____

Your child has had low grades on two or more six-week progress reports. These grades put your child in an at-risk category, meaning that if the poor performance continues there is a possibility of retention next year.

We believe that students in this category have become discouraged, have given up, or feel that they cannot do any better. We will be meeting with them in small groups once a week for the next 10 weeks. Some of the things we will be working on are: how to study, read a chapter, set goals, become involved, and become encouraged rather than discouraged.

You may have reached a point of feeling discouraged, too. You may have tried rewards, punishment, restrictions, anger, or giving up. We are asking for your cooperation in helping your child work toward better grades. Please sit down with your child, away from distractions, and discuss this matter. Attached is a list of suggestions that we encourage you to refer to often. For assistance to be meaningful and result in long-term benefits, there must be a joint effort between home and school.

We would like to invite you to a parent meeting on _____.
At that time we'll briefly explain our program and offer suggestions for you to encourage your child. If you have any questions or want additional information, please call us or your child's teachers.

Sincerely yours,

Counselors

Suggestions for Parents

_____ I will talk with my child privately in an encouraging manner and give assurance that I will be available to help.

_____ Together my child and I will decide on a specific study time and location that is free from distractions.

_____ I will sit down with my child for 10 minutes at the beginning or ending of the study time to review what was learned in each class that day and to find out if homework was assigned.

_____ I realize that school assignments are my child's responsibility and I am not expected to do the homework or project.

_____ I will arrange a conference with my child's teachers or counselor for suggestions on what to do at home.

_____ I will meet with my child at least once a week to discuss his/her progress.

_____ I will initial my child's assignment book on a daily basis.

Group Counseling for School Counselors

Session 2: At-Risk Group

■ *Icebreaker:*

1. My name is . . . and the way I feel about joining this group is . . . and the way I feel about school is . . . (give a number between 1 and 10—1 awful; 10 wonderful).

2. The reason I made bad grades is . . . .

3. Hand out slips of paper to the students, asking them to list, anonymously, all the reasons they make bad grades. Give them five minutes to write the reasons, then pass a basket around for the slips of paper. As you read the reasons, have a student list them on a poster. Discuss each one, and using hand-raises, find out how many students are guilty of each reason. From the list of reasons, ask students to choose one that they would like to improve on this week. Have them write it down on a Student Goal Sheet, then share it aloud with the group.

■ *Skill-Building or Awareness Activity:*

1. Topic: Discouragement. Introduce the topic this way:

    "I don't believe you want to fail. You may think you are so far behind there is no way to catch up. How many of you have become discouraged? How many have given up?

    "Becoming part of this group means you are hopeful that there is a chance for you to improve. I believe you can improve, and together we can work on some skills that will help you in all your subjects. You will have to do the work, make some changes in the way you do things, and, most importantly, commit to attend this group.

    "How many of you agree? How many of you are willing to make some commitments?

    "I'd like to give you this contract to look over. If you agree with what is written here, I'll ask you to sign it. If you feel that you are not able to commit yourself to this contract, you may decide not to be a part of this group."

    Have students fill out Student Contract and discuss what it means.

2. Collect parent letter. Ask students how their parents reacted and if they sat down and discussed the checklist.

■ *Summary:*

Today I learned . . . .

My goal for next week is . . . .

Student Contract

I, _____ , have agreed to join this

group because _____

_____

_____ .

_____ I will attend the group each week.

_____ I will be present at school every day.

_____ I will do my homework each night.

_____ I will use an assignment sheet.

_____ I will use a folder or notebook for each subject.

_____ name

_____ date

Group Counseling for School Counselors

Student Goal Sheets

Name _____ Date _____ Due _____

My goal for this week is to _____

_____

I intend to achieve this goal by _____

_____

Sign _____

Name _____ Date _____ Due _____

My goal for this week is to _____

_____

I intend to achieve this goal by _____

_____

Sign _____

Name _____ Date _____ Due _____

My goal for this week is to _____

_____

I intend to achieve this goal by _____

_____

Sign _____

Session 3: At-Risk Group

■ *Icebreaker:*

My name is . . . and what I have the most trouble with is . . . .
Collect goal sheets and discuss how the week went.

■ *Skill-Building or Awareness Activity:*

1. Ask students: What do you notice about students who do well in school? (List all answers on poster.)

    How many of you know exactly what to do to get your teacher upset? (List answers on other side of poster. Discuss.)

    What are some other ways to be recognized, gain attention, or show power that are not self-defeating?

2. Go over the goals of misbehavior which are based on Alfred Adler's work. Students need to understand the purpose of their misbehavior and better ways to achieve their needs for significance and belonging. (See Dinkmeyer and McKay, *Systematic Training for Effective Teaching—STET*, or a host of other books on Adlerian principles for more details on this important concept.)

■ *Goals of Misbehavior:*

Attention
Power
Revenge
Giving up

Discuss with students how poor academic achievement might be a way to fulfill these goals.

■ *Assignment:*

Name one thing that you can do this week to show your teacher that you want to learn.

Have students write the week's goal on a Student Goal Sheet.

■ *Summary:*

Today I learned . . . .

Session 4: At-Risk Group

■ *Icebreaker:*

I could make better grades if . . . .

■ *Review:*

Students review the goals of misbehavior from last week. Check to see if students met last week's goal. Review assignment: What I did to show my teacher that I wanted to learn . . . .

■ *Skill-Building or Awareness Activity:*

Goal-Setting

1. Introduce tape: *Student Success Training*

   a. This tape presents techniques used by high achievers in sports, school, and business.

   b. Three techniques to pay attention to: relaxation training, goal setting, and picturing success.

   c. Following the tape, you will be asked to write a specific goal and plan to reach it.

2. Play tape after dimming lights and asking students to sit comfortably with eyes closed, heads on desk.

3. After tape, ask students to write goal and plan as directed on tape.

4. Have students share goals and plans. They can divide into groups of 2–4, or share with whole group. Counselor critiques goals and plans as to how clear, definite, and specific they are.

■ *Summary:*

Students write summary of the most important points from this group meeting and several share their summary with class.

■ *Materials:*

Student Success Training, a cassette tape ($14.95). Ocean Publishers, 419 Shorecrest Drive, Clemson, SC 29631.

Name _____ Date _____

Student Success Training Goal Sheet

Course _____

1. My Grade Goal for this course this six weeks is _____ (A, B, C).

2. My *Study Plan*

   Example: To study 20 minutes per day beginning at 4 p.m. in my room at least three days per week. Be sure to include:

   1. amount of time

   2. starting time

   3. where

   4. how many days per week

   My study plan to achieve this goal:

   _____

   _____

   _____

   Goals that are:

   1. clear

   2. have a definite time limit; and

   3. are reasonable

   have the best chance of being achieved. Good luck on reaching your goal.

Session 5: At-Risk Group

■ *Icebreaker:*

One thing I'm getting better at is . . . .

■ *Review:*

Review last week's session on goal setting and check what progress students made on their goals.

■ *Skill-Building or Awareness Activity:*

1. Weekly Goal Sheet and Checklist. Using hand-raises, go through the checklist section of the sheet to see who was present each day, etc. Spend time with each student discussing his/her week. Set the sheet aside for now; you'll come back to it later.

2. Go over "How to Look Smart When You Ask a Question." After completing this section, students write out their goal for the week, focusing on asking questions.

How to Look Smart When You Ask a Question

Students sometimes don't ask questions in class when they don't understand something because they're afraid they'll look dumb. If you know when and how to ask questions, you can look smart even when you don't understand something.

WHEN   Ask: "When are the best times to ask your teacher questions about assignments?" The three recommended times are:

    1. before class;

    2. when the teacher asks, "Are there any questions";

    3. at the end of class.

HOW   The do's and don'ts of asking questions. Ask: "What are some ways to ask questions that might make you look dumb?"

    1. Say "Huh?"

    2. Say "What did you say?"

    3. Ask, "What are we supposed to do?" right after teacher gives instructions.

3. Go over with students the basics of looking good when asking questions:

    1. When asking a question, let the teacher know you heard part of what was said. "Ms. Jones, I understand about . . . and I heard you say . . . , but where I lost you was . . . . Could you say a little more about that?"

    2. Let the teacher know you care. "Mr. Smith, I want to understand this point, but I'm really having a hard time. Could you explain it once more, please?"

        Included in both examples are non-verbal messages—tone of voice, facial expressions, and body language—that must match your verbal message of sincerity in order for your questions to be received positively. (Session 7 focuses on non-verbal communication.)

Name _____ Date _____

Weekly Goal Sheet and Checklist

Week of _____

_____ present every day

_____ not tardy

_____ did homework every day

_____ had supplies (pencil, paper, books)

_____ used assignment book

_____ parents checked assignment book

_____ did classwork every day

Behavior in class

_____ not reprimanded by teacher

_____ once

_____ twice

_____ several times

_____ sent to administration

My goal for the week is _____

_____

_____ .

I intend to complete this goal by _____

_____

_____ .

Accomplished goal

_____ 100%

_____ 75%

_____ 50%

_____ not at all

Session 6: At-Risk Group

■ *Icebreaker:*

I hope . . . .

■ *Review:*

Ask students to tell about their week, and how they are coming on their goals.

■ *Skill-Building or Awareness Activity:*

"Make Sure Each Student:" Handout

Tell students, "I would like to go over with you nine ideas that are helpful to anyone who's interested in doing well in school. Some of these you may already be doing quite well. As we go through these, pick out two or three that you think would help you the most."

1. On number one, students rate themselves 1–10. Ten is great, one is low. Go around circle, sharing ratings.

2. Ask for hand-raises. "How many have a folder or separate section in a notebook for each course? Why is this important? How many have been doing this since we talked about it in session two?"

3–9. Go through remaining items in a similar fashion (1–10 ratings). This is a time for assessment, not getting sidetracked on any one item. End with each member sharing the two or three ideas they think would help most. Ask each student to write a goal for the week.

■ *Summary:*

One thing I learned or relearned today is . . . .

Make Sure Each Student:

1. Is reading and understanding assignments.

2. Has a folder for each class.

3. Writes down homework assignments.

4. Keeps a list of test grades and other grades for each course (in the folder for that class).

5. Has a regular time and place to do homework.

6. Reviews daily assignments—notes daily.

7. Asks for clarification or help when needed (knows how and when to ask).

8. Sets possible, clear, definite goals every week, and keeps up with them.

9. Has a plan for preparing for tests that begins several days in advance.

Session 7: At-Risk Group

■ *Icebreaker:*

Sentence Completions. To introduce communication, have the group respond to the following sentence stems:

When people talk to me, I like for them to . . . .

A time I felt listened to was . . . .

A person who talks all the time makes me feel . . . .

A "put-down" makes me feel . . . .

When people give me unwanted advice, I feel . . . .

I trust people who . . . .

I am willing to listen if . . . .

When I am not listened to, I feel . . . .

■ *Review:*

Review week, goals, and what was observed from teachers' non-verbal behaviors during the previous week.

■ *Skill-Building or Awareness Activity:*

1. Non-Listening Exercise: Have students get into pairs. One student talks for one minute about any topic—favorite movies, pet, hobby, or vacation spot. The other student demonstrates not paying attention, interrupting, and any other non-listening practices. Switch roles, but this time have the other person demonstrate what he considers to be good listening practices. Have the group discuss the behaviors that they noticed with not listening and listening. Have a recorder write down the group's lists of behaviors for both.

   Have the group compare their lists to the ones below.

Listening Behaviors

Eye contact
Interest in other's point of view
Empathy (trying to imagine what the other thinks and feels)
Asking questions to seek clarification
An open, receptive attitude (willingness to change opinion)

The effects of listening usually include a relaxed atmosphere, greater trust, mutual give-and-take.

Non-Listening Behaviors

Paying attention to own ideas first
Trying to convince others you are right
Interrupting others
Speaking in loud voice to overpower other person
Tuning out (not responding)
Lack of eye contact
Not asking questions

The effects of not listening usually include tension, lack of trust, frustration, and a competitive response.

2. Go over Non-Verbal Communication handout. Discuss.

■ **Summary:**

One thing I learned today was . . . .

Ask students to bring social studies book to next meeting.

Name _____ Date _____

Non-Verbal Communication

The communication process is always non-verbal as well as verbal. Behavior expresses meaning, sometimes more clearly than words. To be an effective communicator, one must pay attention to body language and tone of voice. Consider the following:

70% of what we communicate is through body language.
23% of what we communicate is through tone of voice.
7% of what we communicate is through words.

How we say something is frequently more important than what we say.

If you're interested in improving your non-verbal communication skills, follow these do's and don'ts.

	Do's	*Don'ts*
Eyes	good eye contact	stare, glare, jittery, no eye contact
Voice (volume)	loud enough to be heard clearly	too soft or too loud
Voice (tone)	tone communicates understanding	disinterested, gruff tone, sarcastic
Facial expressions	matches your own or other's feeling; smile	frown, yawn, sigh, scowl, blank look
Posture	leaning forward slightly, relaxed	leaning away, rigid, slouching, crossing arms
Movement	toward	away
Distance	arm's length	too close (less than 2 feet); too far (more than 5 feet)

Group Counseling for School Counselors

Session 8: At-Risk Group

■ *Icebreaker:*

One way my non-verbal behavior this week showed my teacher I was interested was . . . .

■ *Review:*

Students review their week, goals.

■ *Skill-Building or Awareness Activity:*

1. "How to Approach Any Reading Assignment" handout. Go over the handout with students.

2. Leader guides students through upcoming social-studies chapter, using the reading handout.

■ *Summary:*

One thing I learned or relearned today is . . . .

Ask students to write goal for upcoming week. Ask students to bring math books next week.

Name _____ Date _____

How to Approach Any Reading Assignment

There are many helpful methods of improving reading comprehension. We recommend that you have a clear step-by-step approach that can be easily followed.

1. Develop an overview of the reading. Ask yourself, "What are this section's key points?" To begin to get the "big picture" of what the section is about:

   • Look at any pictures, graphs—read captions.

   • Read introduction paragraph and summary paragraph.

   • Read questions, if any, at end of section.

   • Look over vocabulary list.

   • Look at boldface headings. Turn each heading into a question you will answer when you read the section.

2. Read the section. As you read, mentally answer the questions you made up from each heading. Make a list of any terms you don't understand. As you finish each sub-section, mentally summarize the main ideas.

3. Review what you have read. Look over questions and key terms at end of section. If you cannot answer them, return to the section where they are covered and reread. Before leaving the section, be sure you can answer the *W* and *H* questions: who, what, when, where, why, and how.

The chart below summarizes these steps and indicates the percentage of comprehension we gain as we progress through each step.

■ *How to Make Remembering What You Read Easier*

Preview 10–20% Comprehension	*Read* 50–80% Comprehension	*Review* 85–98% Comprehension
1. Look at pictures, graphs, charts—read captions.	1. Read to answer questions.	1. Go back to questions and try to answer mentally.
2. Read summary and questions.	2. Write down any boldface words or terms you don't understand.	2. For those you can't answer, refer back to text.
3. Read the headings, turning them into questions.	3. After finishing each heading, mentally summarize.	3. Make sure you answer all the *W* and *H* questions.

Session 9: At-Risk Group

■ *Icebreaker:*

One reading tip I used this week was . . . .

■ *Review:*

Students review their week and goal sheet.

■ *Skill-Building or Awareness Activity:*

Math Tutoring handout. Ask students to generate current problems in math. Process the handout, using the particular problems they bring up in the math book. Have students get into pairs, going through the math problem and the handout.

Note: The handout can be used by the group leader or by a student tutor. An at-risk program could involve tutoring by students who have had training in how to tutor.

■ *Summary:*

Today I learned . . . .

Math Tutoring

1. Pinpoint the type of math problems on which the student is having difficulty.

2. Ask the student to choose a problem and begin working. As the student begins, ask him to say out loud each step he is performing.

3. When the student cannot specify what he should do next or gives the wrong step, stop. Help the student find an example with an explanation in the text. Ask him to read this example step by step out loud.

4. If no clear example is available, the tutor writes out the necessary steps. Ask the student to try the original problem again, using the steps presented.

5. If the tutor is not able to find clear steps in text or write them from memory, the tutor should see the student's teacher for help in clarifying steps.

In general, working math problems involves applying a series of steps in a set order. Therefore it is helpful for the student to a) write the steps, b) say the steps as he performs each operation, checking them off as he goes.

Many difficulties in math occur because students have not mastered the basic four computations—adding, subtracting, multiplying, and dividing.

Tutors should check these basic computations when they notice errors being made. When a deficit in a computation skill is observed, flash cards and sample problems to build the deficient skills are used.

Session 10: At-Risk Group

■ *Icebreaker:*

The most helpful part of this group has been . . . .

■ *Review:*

Review week, goals, assignment sheet.

■ *Skill-Building or Awareness Activity:*

1. Compare grades from before group to present time. Discuss their progress.

2. Have students complete a written evaluation. Discuss.

3. Address envelope to parents that contains letter to inform them that the group is over.

■ *Summary:*

What I need to do is . . . .

Discuss individual follow-up with the counselor and a monthly support group.

Parents of _____ ,

    Your child has just completed a ten-week group course for students who are at risk academically. During these sessions we have covered such topics as: talking with your teacher, goal setting, reasons students fail, how parents can encourage, and strategies to change negative behavior.

    The majority of the students have found the course to be beneficial and have improved their grades. We will meet with them once a month for the remainder of the year. We ask for your continued support in working with your child.

                                                  Sincerely yours,

                                                  Counselor

                                                  Counselor

Frequency Table

It is useful to tally how many students brought their grades up and share this with teachers and parents. A frequency table is helpful. A sample is shown below.

Total number of students in at-risk group: _____

Criterion for selection:

Number who brought at least one subject up at
least one letter grade: _____

                                           percent of total _____

Number who brought two subjects up at
least one letter grade: _____

                                           percent of total _____

Number who brought three or more subjects up at
least one letter grade: _____

                                           percent of total _____

Optional Activities

1. Coopersmith Self-Concept Inventory. Depending on how long the group meets and what your goals are, you may want to administer a self-concept survey. We use the *Coopersmith Self-Concept Inventory* at the beginning of the group, and again at the end of the year.

2. Learning-Styles Inventory. Find a learning-styles inventory that determines whether students are auditory, visual, or kinesthetic learners. We use the one that is computer administered and divided into 10 categories. For more information, write to MAC Ware, P.O. Box 27, Chillicothe, OH 45601.

3. Role-play: One student volunteers to be the teacher teaching a social-studies lesson from the book. Each student is given a role on a piece of paper. Some roles are: quiet, interrupting, thumping pencil, always raising hand, talking out loud. (We strongly recommend that you have students role-play only the "good guys" if the role-play involves any controversial issues or illegal activities.) Roles are repeated, depending on size of group. The student who plays the role of teacher discovers how frustrating it is to be a teacher. Students can switch roles as long as there is time. Group discussion focuses on what is your role as a student.

4. Project yourself into the future and pretend that you have children. What three things would you like to teach or give your children? Think of things that your parents do that you like and want to continue, and things that you as a parent would want to avoid doing. What do your parents do to encourage your learning?

5. Consider having a guest speaker talk to the group about his/her experiences. If the grade level you are working with will be going to high school next year, have a high-school counselor talk to the group. The counselor could also bring a student who had difficulties at the beginning of high school but straightened up and became successful.

6. Another source is the book *You Can Be President* by Bob Moore. These stories feature famous people who tried many times before becoming successful. These stories are very encouraging. We like to routinely do a read-around with one of these stories. Each story focuses on motivation, determination, and not giving up.

Supplemental Guide for Group Leaders

■ *Study Skills Tips*

1. How to improve concentration and memory

   a. Space out review rather than cram.

   b. Relax.

   c. Focus on key terms—create outline.

   d. Use memory techniques for key terms, i.e., acronyms.

   e. Make information meaningful.

      1. Ask questions.
      2. Find something interesting.
      3. Anticipate questions teacher will ask.

   f. Use several types of learning.

      1. Reading
      2. Writing
      3. Listening
      4. Speaking

2. Preparing for tests

   a. Read material and take notes.

   b. Answer questions; put key terms in notes.

   c. Boil class and reading notes down to 1–2 pages.

   d. Go over these 1–2 pages 5–10 times, spaced over 2–3 days.

   e. Find out all you can about the test.

      1. What kind—i.e., short answer, multiple-choice, essay, matching, etc.
      2. Make up a practice test.
      3. Ask your teacher about the test.

   f. No new reading within 24 hours of test, if possible. Instead, have notes organized by night before and only review.

   g. Picture yourself doing well.

3. Taking tests

   a. Use slow breathing to relax.

   b. Look over test; answer easy ones first.

   c. Go back to hard item; look for clues; eliminate wrong answers; take educated guess.

   d. Go for items with most points first.

   e. Budget your time.

■ *Study Skills Tips (continued)*

4. How to avoid test anxiety

   a. Overlearn the details, facts.

   b. Know all you can about the test—see #2(e) above.

   c. Use a practice test—make up your own or ask teacher.

   d. Have a test-taking strategy and follow it—see #3 above.

   e. Imagine yourself taking the test and doing well.

   f. During the test, use nickel-breathing technique: breathe in slowly to count of 5; hold for 5 counts; exhale slowly to 5 counts; repeat 5 times.

Resources for At-Risk Groups

Bednar, R.L., and S.L. Weinberg. "Ingredients of Successful Treatment Programs for Underachievers." *Journal of Counseling Psychology, 17,* pp. 1–7, 1970.

Brigman, Greg. "Student Success Training," a cassette tape on study skills, goal-setting, relaxation training, and motivation. Ocean Publishers, Clemson University, College of Education, Tillman Hall, Clemson, SC 29634-0709.

Caliste, E.R. (1980). *The Effect of Counseling on the Behavior of Sixth Grade Underachievers.* (ERIC Document Reproduction Service No. ED 194 823)

Coopersmith, S. *Self-Esteem Inventories.* Palo Alto, Consulting Psychologists Press, 1986.

Larsen, Pam and Bruce Shertzer. "The High School Dropout: Everybody's Problem." *The School Counselor, 34,* pp. 163–169, 1987.

Mahan, C., and Johnson, C. "Portrait of a Dropout: Dealing with Academic, Social and Emotional Problems." *NASSP Bulletin, 67,* pp. 80–83, 1983.

Morse, Linda A. "Working with Young Procrastinators: Elementary School Students Who Do Not Complete School Assignments." *Elementary School Guidance and Counseling, 21,* 221–228, Feb. 1987.

Slavin, R. E. (1989). "What Works for Students At Risk: A Research Synthesis." *Educational Leadership, 46(5),* 4–13.

Thompson, Rosemary. "Creating Instructional and Counseling Partnerships to Improve Academic Performance of Underachievers." *The School Counselor, 34,* 289–294, 1987.

Wilson, N.S. "Counselor Interventions with Low-Achieving and Underachieving Elementary, Middle and High School Students: A Review of the Literature." *Journal of Counseling and Development, 64,* 628–634, 1986.

Buddy System

Grade Level: High School	
Time Required: Seven Sessions	
Author: Gayl Kelly	

The purpose of this group is to team a senior who previously had difficulties in school—such as academic failure, attendance, and/or peer relationships—with a freshman having similar difficulties.

■ *Goals and Objectives:*

- To aid freshmen/seniors in enhancing self-esteem
- To improve peer relationships
- To give students a better understanding of skills necessary for a successful high school career
- To improve the communication skills of the seniors and freshmen
- To improve students' academic performance
- To facilitate students' ability to request help when needed
- To help students recognize problem areas and seek appropriate help
- To encourage student participation in extra-curricular/community activities
- To help students access their feelings and better understand them
- To help students recognize how the need for approval shapes behavior, thoughts, feelings, and actions
- To facilitate sharing ideas for success

■ *Method:*

- Request names of freshmen and seniors from teachers, administrators, and counselors.
- Ask seniors if they would like to be a buddy. Ask freshmen if they would like to have a buddy. (Seniors participating in the Buddy System frequently have had previous training as peer helpers. In addition, they will have 2–5 training sessions according to their need. Ongoing training as the program progresses is provided that is tailored to the specific needs of the Buddies, i.e., tutoring skills, encouragement skills, and listening/problem-solving skills. For a listing of specific peer-training materials, see the resources listed at the end of this section.)

- Team the senior and the freshman based on the information available (sex, same number of courses failed, attendance problems, similar home situations, etc.) so that a common bond can be more readily formed.

- Give a permission slip to both seniors and freshmen, and relate details and purpose of the program.

- After permission slips have been returned, issue a group pass to each student.

■ *Logistics:*

Sessions 1 and 2 should take place in the same month. Sessions 3, 4, and 5 should take place once a month. Sessions 6 and 7 should take place in the same month. All group sessions after Session 1 include seniors and their freshman buddies.

The primary activity will occur between seniors and freshmen outside of group sessions. The basic assumption is that the freshmen will listen, relate to, and incorporate information from the seniors more readily than from "just one more adult." The meetings may occur in any number of locations, such as the peer counselor/leader room, media center, classroom after school, the individuals' homes, or perhaps a local favorite such as McDonald's or Burger King.

The purpose of the group sessions is to bring together these individuals and introduce activities that will stimulate ideas that they can use for themselves or with their buddy. The activities are experiential and designed to have the students use various methods of identifying and solving problems.

The counselor may wish to have both freshmen and seniors meet together for all sessions. If this is done, the counselor needs to schedule separate meetings for the freshmen and seniors at least every other month.

The purpose of having freshmen and seniors meeting separately is to have time to process the buddy meetings without the buddy being present. It has been found that problems may be occurring and the buddy does not address the issue because the other buddy is present. Also, buddies may simply feel that it is not a problem of any major concern that needs to be addressed to the group. However, if a session is limited to just freshmen or just seniors, these problems can be addressed. The counselor must ask for concerns of the group members: Does their buddy seem to be giving too much advice, or is he/she not keeping appointments with them? Once the conversation begins, both positive and negative comments are expressed concerning the buddies—the group process begins so that the others can offer what has worked for them or say that the problem also exists for them.

The counselor may wish to have every other session one in which freshmen and seniors meet separately. Any number of arrangements can be used so that not only is the cohesiveness of the group members considered but also the need for discussion of their buddies without hesitation or embarrassment.

Seniors will be required to keep a log or calendar to record contacts with the buddy. Seniors may contact the counselor at any time to discuss buddy or to ask for additional study information.

■ *Testing:*

The Buddy System is designed to start a few weeks after the beginning of a semester and conclude a few weeks before the end of that same semester. Therefore, all pre-assessments of attendance and grades are based on the previous semester. All post-assessments are based on the final grades and attendance of the current semester.

A pre-behavior rating scale and self-esteem inventory, such as the Cooper-Smith Self-Esteem Inventory, should be distributed/administered at the beginning of the group (preferably *before* Session 1) and the post-assessments of the same should be distributed/administered at the conclusion of the group sessions.

Seniors—Pre- and Post-Assessments
   Grades
   Self-esteem

Freshmen—Pre- and Post-Assessments
   Grades
   Self-esteem
   Attendance
   Behavior Rating Scale

Data on the freshmen are necessary for the accountability of the group. The additional data on the seniors are optional, but may provide pertinent information concerning the effectiveness of the program for seniors as well as freshmen.

Session 1: Buddy System

For the first session, meet with seniors separately and then meet with freshmen.

■ *Purpose:*

To review the purpose of the group

To establish ground rules

To introduce members to one another

To allow members to feel comfortable with others by discussing common interests from introductions

To elicit feelings concerning Buddy System

To list freshmen problem areas

To give seniors guidelines for being a successful buddy

■ *Introduction:*

Begin by explaining the purpose of the Buddy System and the group rules (confidentiality, attendance, no put-downs, and one person talking at a time). Also explain that whether in large-group session or in buddy session, the peer must report to the counselor and the counselor must report any information which might be viewed as a threat or potential threat to the life of the individual or another (this includes but is not limited to suicide; drug abuse; physical, emotional, or sexual abuse; or threats on the life of another) by the policy set forth by the local school.

Use the following activity to introduce group members to one another and to facilitate group cohesiveness.

■ *Skill-Building or Awareness Activity:*

The Interview

1. Have students get into pairs. Supply each person with a sheet of paper and pencil. The first person interviews the second person so that the first person can introduce the second person to the group. (Allow three to four minutes.) Then the second person interviews the first person.

    When interviews are complete, begin with a volunteer to introduce his/her partner to the group. Continue around the circle. (Leader may preface activity by stating that we probably all feel uncomfortable introducing ourselves, so we will allow someone else to help us.)

2. From information gleaned from introductions, discuss similarities among group members. Continue discussion with the following questions:

    How do you feel about being chosen for the program?

    How do you feel about the nature of the program?

    Seniors: What do you think you can contribute to this freshman?

    Freshmen: What information or help do you want from this senior?

3. **Seniors:** Go over some of the techniques of information giving. Remind them not to give advice. Review use of I-messages, as opposed to you-messages; listening skills; use of feeling words. Supply seniors with a list of feeling words as well as a packet of study skills/test-taking information, log, and any other materials suitable for use. (See "At-Risk Group" plans for specific ideas on pages 177–204).

   Freshmen: Have students make a list of the problems they encountered last semester that interfered with their academic/social success. What problems are they now encountering? Process their responses as a group and encourage them to share their responses with their senior buddies. (Leader writes problems on poster board to use in Session 6.)

■ *Summary:*

Review similarities from introductions. Briefly restate ground rules. **Freshmen:** Have them review the kind of help they hope to receive from buddy. **Seniors:** Have them review the kind of help they hope to give buddy.

Double-check on names with "Goodbye _____ " activity. Ask each student to turn to the person on the right and say goodbye and then that person's name. Repeat process with the person on the left.

■ *Homework:*

Seniors: Keep a record of sessions with buddy; include weekly grades, attendance, and goal. Remember the criteria established for the recording of sessions. (Give them a copy of the criteria, found on the next page.)

Freshmen: Keep a record of weekly grades and attendance.

Criteria for a Senior Meeting with a Freshman Buddy

1. There should be a meeting twice a week, preferably at the beginning of the week and near the end of the week. Occasionally, the meeting time may be limited to only once a week due to schedules and other difficulties. This should not occur more than twice for the entire length of the group session.

2. Seniors may use their scheduled meeting time for peer counseling, tutoring, support, or just building a rapport. Any problems such as abuse (within the family, or the individual abusing self or substances), suicide, or other major areas of concern should always be reported to the counselor immediately.

3. Seniors should feel free to consult with the counselor, teacher, or other professional support staff to obtain material, information, or support for helping their buddy. (They may ask the counselor for material for test-taking skills, a teacher for information regarding problem-solving techniques for a particular subject area, the media specialist for tutoring materials.)

4. Seniors will keep a record of their sessions with their buddy. The record should consist of the following items:

    date

    time and location of the session

    brief summary of the session (general information such as tutoring session in math, peer counseling on boyfriend problem, etc.)

    the next scheduled session's time, date, and location as well as the senior's anticipated topic for that session

5. Seniors will give the record of these sessions to the Buddy System counselor at scheduled meetings or as directed by the counselor at times other than scheduled meetings. The counselor may wish to keep the record or simply review and return it to the senior.

Session 2: Buddy System

Note: Both seniors and freshmen attend this session. Paper and pencils are necessary. Light snacks would also be appropriate.

■ *Purpose:*

To introduce the freshmen and seniors

To illustrate that we all have common likes and interests

To introduce buddy pairs

To exchange information within buddy pairs so that the Buddy System can begin

To enjoy one another's company by using activity and snacks as a means of reducing tension

■ *Introduction:*

Welcome both freshmen and seniors. Begin by stating purpose and ground rules. Preface activity by stating that the activity will help us relax with one another and learn some interesting things about one another.

■ *Skill-Building or Awareness Activity:*

Double Line

1. Begin by forming a double line with an equal number of students on both sides. Each line alternates seniors and freshmen. Each set of partners has 14 seconds to answer a question, 7 seconds each. ("Stop" will be called after 7 seconds as a signal to switch. Then "Move one person" will be called and the line on the right of the leader moves ahead one person (end person comes around to other end). Here are possible questions:

    If you could spend an hour with a famous person, who would it be and why?

    If you had to live somewhere else for a year, where would it be?

    Who is your hero/heroine and why?

    If you had to change your first name, what would the new one be and why?

    What is one thing about school you like and one thing you dislike?

    What subject in school are you best at and why?

    What is one thing that makes you happy and why?

    What is your favorite (tv program, food, musical group, pastime, color, season, etc.) and why?

    If you had to move to Pakistan next year, what would you miss most about the place where you now live?

What one change would you most like to see in our society?

Allow the line to move completely through at least one time (more if you have time and see that the group is really enjoying the activity).

2. Discuss any similarities among students. Ask them to raise hands if their partner started a topic they would like to go back and discuss some more, or that they found interesting or funny. Remind them that making new friends is often very easy once you have something to talk about or share. The buddy system will give them an opportunity to share with one another.

■ *Exchange of names:*

Call names of buddy pairs. Ask students to write down their buddy's full name, address, phone number, schedule of classes and teachers (room numbers if possible), and list of after-school events in which they are participating (include days and practice times).

■ *Summary:*

After giving the buddy pairs ample time to exchange information, ask the group to remember that confidentiality extends into the buddy sessions with one another. Encourage them to continue with fellowship. Give homework assignment. Enjoy snacks and mingle.

■ *Homework:*

Same as assignment from Session 1. Tell groups to wear slacks or shorts to next meeting.

Session 3: Buddy System

■ *Purpose:*

To allow members to work cooperatively

To have group members experience qualities necessary for a positive working relationship

To be able to visualize and vocalize problems and solutions

To be able to ask others for their help and cooperation

To improve peer relationships.

■ *Icebreaker:*

Ask students to state their name and the problem areas in which they are working with their buddies. Allow for questions and any information-giving, as necessary.

■ *Skill-Building or Awareness Activity:*

Entanglement

1. Students form a circle, arms crossed and outstretched in front of them. Each student reaches into center of circle and grasps the hands of two people. (Make sure they are holding the hands of people other than those standing next to them.) Without releasing their grip, they must untangle the knot formed by the group. They should end up in a circle; however, some may be facing inward and some outward.

2. Ask the following questions: How did you feel at different times when untangling the knot? Use feeling words. (Confused, no direction, confident, excited when accomplished.) What were some of the qualities of the people that helped untangle the group? Use feeling words. (Cooperation, leadership, acceptance, willingness to try.) Relate these qualities to the buddy system.

■ *Summary:*

Ask each person to state a feeling that came to them while tangling/untangling that might be a benefit in the process of helping/being helped by their buddy. Example: I need to be more accepting; buddy needs to be more excited about learning; etc.

Session 4: Buddy System

■ *Purpose:*

To become aware of feelings

To become aware of our need for approval

To facilitate understanding of how our need for approval affects our thoughts and behaviors.

■ *Icebreaker:*

Have students share with group successes with or concerns about buddy. Ask them to share how they or their buddy used what was learned in the last session.

■ *Skill-Building or Awareness Activity:*

"I Am."

1. This exercise is a series of unfinished statements. With the group in a circle, whip around the room, having each member complete a different sentence with whatever comes to mind. Allow for a second or third round if participants are interested. Another alternative is to throw out several of the statements to the group as a whole. A discussion or elaboration may follow.

> I'm happiest when . . . .
> In a group, I am . . . .
> When I'm alone at home, I . . . .
> Most people I know . . . .
> I get angry when . . . .
> What I want most in my life is . . . .
> I often find myself . . . .
> People who know me well think I am . . . .
> I used to be . . . .
> It makes me uncomfortable when . . . .
> When people first meet me, they . . . .
> When someone tries to bully me, I feel . . . .
> When I'm on cloud nine, I feel . . . .
> When someone praises my work, I feel . . . .
> When I'm on a blind date, I feel . . . .
> When people don't appreciate what I have done, I feel . . . .
> When everyone is telling me what to do, I feel . . . .
> When I'm loved, I feel . . . .
> I have never liked . . . .
> I trust those who . . . .
> In a group, I am most afraid of . . . .
> I respect . . . .
> I feel irritated when . . . .
> From past experiences, I believe teachers think I am . . . .
> My family thinks that I am . . . .

What I like best at school is . . . .
Usually when the teacher calls on me, I feel . . . .
I would consider it risky to . . . .
I need to improve most in . . . .
It makes me proud . . . .
A good thing that happened recently was . . . .
Since last year, I have changed most in . . . .
Usually I don't like to talk about . . . .
People seem to like my . . . .

2. Ask "Did any of you not say exactly your first thought because you were concerned with what others might think—that they might not approve of you or what you thought? Discuss how you felt when you realized your first reaction might not be approved by others. We all want the approval of others. How does this affect our conduct in class, study habits, projects, participation in class discussions, etc.? Do we always seek approval in positive ways? How so?

"How does this discussion help you see yourself and help you relate to your buddy?"

■ *Summary:*

Review the session, using students' statements about approval. Ask them to keep this session's discussion in mind while they silently respond to the following statement:

Approval from others is more important to me than my own self-approval. (Respond with strongly agree; agree; neutral; disagree; or strongly disagree.)

Ask students to consider how their response relates to the way they approach academic/social activities (positive or negative). Ask them to keep their response in mind the next time a situation arises in which they withhold their first response or reaction (either positive or negative).

■ *Homework:*

Write on paper an incident in which you changed your answer or behavior because of what others might think.

Session 5: Buddy System

■ *Purpose:*

To visualize problems

To ask for cooperation in changing problem areas

To actually change a problem after recognizing it as such

To improve peer relationships

To facilitate a feeling of self-worth by handling problem areas successfully

To facilitate sharing ideas for success

To improve communication skills by having others follow verbal directions

To identify feelings when visualizing problem areas

■ *Icebreaker:*

Ask for any questions or concerns. Share homework assignment (how we changed answer or action because of what others might think). Have group discuss any common feelings or incidents.

■ *Skill-Building or Awareness Activity:*

Body Sculptures

1. Introduce the concept of body sculptures. Using group members, sculpt a problem. (Example: A student talks to friend on phone while doing homework in living room, where his little brother plays a video game.) Place group members to show this scene. Discuss how you can actually see how this arrangement of people interferes with learning/studying. Resculpt with friend waiting until student finishes homework, student in another room at comfortable studying area/position, and brother playing video in living room. (This is a suggestion. Try to elicit a real problem from the group and sculpt it.)

2. Encourage other group members to discuss what is going on. Example: Can you see anything that interferes with the student's studying? Can you see why his study efforts are being defeated? How can this be changed? Do it!

3. Some problems may not lend themselves readily to sculpting, but an effort can be made. The idea is to visualize a problem and then change its direction. Others can learn from how a person changes his or her own personal situation.

4. How did it feel to share the success of a problem conquered? How did it feel to "look" at the problem? Could you "see" why a situation might be difficult? When the situation changed, could you see as well as feel that the change was positive?

Summary:

Review what was learned in today's activity. Encourage group to visualize problems so that they can better work solutions. Suggest a problem area that they might work on next.

Homework:

Ask group to mentally sculpt a problem and then sculpt a solution. Ask them to write down the problem, the parts that contribute to the problem, and the solutions taken. Example:

Problem: Poor grades on homework.

Parts that contribute: Friend on phone, brother in same room, etc.

Solution: Have friend call later, study in own room or when brother is finished with game.

Suggest that visualizing a problem by sculpting with people or visualizing it on paper helps facilitate better solutions.

Session 6: Buddy System

■ *Purpose:*

To facilitate sharing of ideas for success

To identify one's own feelings and better understand them

To better understand skills necessary for a successful high school career

To enhance self-esteem

■ *Icebreaker:*

This is the last group session. Begin by sharing successes great and small. **Freshmen:** How has your buddy helped you the most? **Seniors:** How has your buddy improved? Do you think this is a worthwhile project? Why or why not? Any suggestions for the next group of buddies?

■ *Skill-Building or Awareness Activity:*

1. **Freshmen:** Bring out the list of problem areas from Session 1—cross off the successes. Ask students: How does it feel to cross off some of the areas? How does it feel if some areas are still left? (Words such as hopeful, small obstacles, inconvenient but obtainable, etc. will probably be used in discussing areas still left.)
   Seniors: Go over some of the communication skills taught in Session 1. Ask each senior how he/she used these skills with buddy.

2. Discuss: How does it feel to have the group sessions over, as well as the buddy system? How can you use what you have learned now that the program is over? (Encourage lots of feeling words.)

Summary:

Each person takes a turn at the sentence stem: "At the beginning of the Buddy System I . . . but now I . . . . " Process the feelings from the stem. Give invitation to the total group get-together (Session 7).

Homework:

Bring a goodie to share for the get-together.

Session 7: Buddy System

■ *Purpose:*

To improve peer relationships

To facilitate sharing ideas for success

To provide an opportunity for mutual thanks

To encourage participation in extracurricular/community activities

To enhance self-esteem

To formally end the group sessions of the Buddy System

Note: Both freshmen and seniors attend this meeting. Provide a large circle of chairs, pencils, and "You're Terrific" sheets. Buddy sits next to buddy.

■ *Icebreaker:*

Begin by stating that this is the final session of the Buddy System. Ask each buddy to say his/her own name and how he/she feels about helping or having been helped. Encourage open discussion—point out similar problems and successes among buddy pairs.

■ *Skill-Building or Awareness Activity:*

1. Give each person a pen or pencil and a "You're Terrific" sheet. Ask buddies to write each other a thank-you note, mentioning specific instances that helped them or that they enjoyed. After notes are written, ask them to hold the notes until the conclusion of the session.

2. Discuss: How did you feel as you wrote the note? (Awkward, too much to say and not enough paper, embarrassed, nothing to say, etc.) Would you recommend that the Buddy System be used again? Why or why not? List on paper the pros and cons.

   Read pros and cons aloud after all the contributions have been made. Ask if the group agrees. Discuss with the group whether the Buddy System should be used again.

■ *Summary:*

Ask each student to finish with a word or two of praise for his/her buddy (helpful, energetic, cooperative, knowledgeable, tries, works hard, creative, responsible, loads of patience, etc.). After all have had a chance to praise their buddy, the "You're Terrific" notes are exchanged. As they exchange notes, encourage them to share successes as they snack on refreshments and enjoy the fellowship of all the buddies.

■ *Homework:*

Ask the group members to remember the lessons presented and to continue working on more successes. Since most of them have enjoyed the group, encourage them to become active in extracurricular/community activities. These activities will provide continued enjoyment, friendship and success.

You're Terrific!

Group Counseling for School Counselors

Dear Parent,

At _____ High School we are constantly trying to improve our services to students and parents. Your son or daughter has been selected for a pilot study-skills project which will involve administering a self-esteem inventory. The group will be conducted by a counselor skilled in this area.

If you have any questions, or do not want your child involved in this project, please inform me by calling xxx-xxxx.

Sincerely,

Counselor

My son or daughter, _____ , has my permission to attend the pilot study-skills project. I understand that my student will miss no more than one class period of each subject (the group will rotate the meeting through the six class periods). The student is responsible for obtaining work that he/she will miss due to the group meeting.

_____   _____
              · Signature   Date

SAMPLE PASS TO "BUDDY" GROUP

Dear

    This is your pass to the group meetings on the below listed dates. Please check in with your teacher and then come directly to the counselor's office. We will start right after the bell. Please have your teacher initial this pass before coming to group.

Session #1	Wednesday, (month, day)	1st period
2		2nd period
3		3rd period
4		4th period
5		5th period
6		6th period
7		TBA

See you Wednesday.

    Counselor

(*NOTE:* Many teachers find it very helpful to have the exact day the students will be absent from their class. They record it on their attendance register and find that on some days, due to various school functions, activities, group meetings, pre-arranged absences, etc., that they would be wise to plan an alternate lesson rather than have a majority of students miss an important lecture or test. This is helpful in creating a cooperative atmosphere between teachers and the counseling department.]

Name _____ Date _____

I understand:

_____ That I have made a commitment to attend the group for consecutive sessions.

_____ That attendance will be taken in group and it is my responsibility to report to the group room and be ready to begin on time.

_____ That it is my responsibility to make arrangements in advance with classroom teachers for any work that I may miss by being in group.

_____ That it is my responsibility to keep what others say and do in group confidential.

_____ That the group leaders will also keep confidential what I say and do in group, involving other people only when they become concerned for my health, safety, or welfare.

_____ That all school policies regarding acceptable behavior apply to the group.

_____ That I am responsible for completing all assignments that are part of the group.

Signed: _____
                        (Student)

Test Tips

■ *Physical Readiness*

1. Get a good night's sleep.
2. Eat a nourishing breakfast.
3. Wear comfortable clothing and dress for the temperature of the room you will be taking the test in.
4. Do not take tranquilizers or stimulants.
5. If you are supposed to wear glasses, wear them. This is no time for vanity.

■ *Reduce Anxiety*

1. Be on time.
2. Don't rush through the test, but don't dally either.
3. Don't worry about the whole test at once—tackle questions one at a time.
4. Don't "score" yourself as you take the test.
5. Don't look for letter patterns of correct answers.
6. Don't panic if you have a memory lapse or mental block. This is a normal occurrence. Go on to the next item and come back to the trouble spot later.
7. Don't expect to *know* the answer to every question. Expect some items to be too hard. Just do your best.
8. Avoid unnecessary clock-watching, but do be aware of the time.
9. Ignore other test takers.
10. Don't sit near your friends.
11. Think positively.
12. Don't give up!

■ *Follow Directions*

1. Read all directions carefully.
2. Do the sample questions even though you think you understand.
3. If you don't completely understand what to do, don't hesitate to ask for clarification.
4. Sometimes you will need to reread the directions or the questions to be sure you are answering what is being asked.
5. Don't assume that all the questions in the same section follow the same pattern. One question may ask for a true statement, the next may ask which statement is *not* true.
6. Don't guess wildly on a question. Try to eliminate one or two choices to a question. If you guess, make an "educated guess."

Test Tips *(continued)*

■ *Time Management*

1. Read the questions first, then read the paragraph.

2. Understand that reading to answer specific questions is a different task than reading for content mastery.

3. Answer the easiest questions first.

4. Skip over the more difficult items and come back to them later. List these numbers on scratch paper and be sure to skip that row on your answer sheet.

Resources for the Buddy System

Bowman. "Special Focus on Peer Helpers." *Elementary School Guidance and Counseling*, 18 (1983), pp. 109–146.

Brigman and Earley. *Peer Helping: A Training Guide.* J. Weston Walch, Publisher, Portland, ME, 1990.

Dinkmeyer and McKay. *STET: Systematic Training for Effective Teaching.* American Guidance Service, Minneapolis, MN, 1980.

Gazda, Walters, and Childers. *Real Talk: Exercises in Friendship and Helping Skills.* Humanics Limited, Atlanta, GA, 1981.

Georgia Department of Education. *Personal Education: Middle School Seminar Series.* Atlanta, GA, 1982.

Georgia Department of Education. *Psychological Education: Middle School Seminar Series.* Atlanta, GA, 1982.

Gordon. *PET: Parent Effectiveness Training.* New American Library, New York, 1970.

Government Printing Office. *Occupational Outlook Handbook, 1988–1989.* Washington, DC, 1988.

Gray and Tindall. *Peer Counseling.* Accelerated Development, Muncie, IN, 1978.

Kalb and Viscott. *What Every Kid Should Know.* Houghton Mifflin, Boston, 1974.

Myrick. *Development Guidance and Counseling: A Practical Approach.* Educational Media, Minneapolis, MN, 1987.

Myrick and Bowman. *Children Helping Children: Teaching Students to Become Friendly Helpers.* Educational Media, Minneapolis, MN, 1981.

Myrick and Bowman. *Youth Helping Youth* (a 27-minute film). Educational Media, Minneapolis, MN, Educational Media, 1987.

National Peer Helpers Association. For information, write Dr. Don Sorenson, NPHA Treasurer, 1712 Colonial Dr., Cape Girardeau, MO 63701.

Scholastic Book Services, *Choices* booklet series. For information, write Scholastic, Inc., 730 Broadway, New York, NY 10003.

Treat. *TLC: Talking, Listening, Communicating.* Pro-Ed, Austin, TX, 1982.

Verwers. "A Peer Program in Action." *Peer Facilitator Quarterly*, 2(3)(1985), p. 8.

Walton. *Winning Teenagers Over.* Practical Psychology Associates, Chicago, IL, 1980.

Pregnancy Education/Support Group

Grade Level: Middle School and High School	
Time Required: Six Sessions	
Author: Maryanne Brannigan Grimes	

■ *Group Objectives:*

To provide factual information on the birthing process to pregnant teens

To educate students about options and alternatives available to pregnant teens

To provide a safe atmosphere for pregnant teens to explore their feelings concerning their pregnancy

■ *Time:*

Each group session lasts one class period and will last for six sessions.

More sessions can be added if the leader so desires.

■ *Group Composition:*

The group is composed of 7 to 10 pregnant teens. (Statistics show that 50% of all pregnant teens drop out of school. I have found this to be true. For this reason, teen mothers might be invited to join.)

■ *Group Rules:*

1. Everything that is said is confidential.

2. No question is stupid.

3. Don't press your values/beliefs on other group members.

Session 1: Pregnancy Group

■ *Icebreaker:*

Grape Activity. Give each student a grape. Have them examine it and get to know it. Then have them put the grapes back in a bowl. Shake them up and ask the students to find "their" grape. Usually they aren't sure if they're finding the right grape. It's difficult to know someone unless you learn about him or her—looking at the surface isn't always enough.

■ *Skill-Building or Awareness Activity:*

1. Hand out the "Get Acquainted" sheets.

2. Allow students 5 minutes to complete sheets.

3. Have students form dyads and discuss their answers with their partners.

4. After sufficient time has passed, have students form a circle and introduce their partner to the group.

5. Talk about group rules. If students would like to add another one or two, allow them to do so. Keep the rules simple.

6. Going around the circle, have students complete the statement, "I hope to get/ gain/learn _____ from this group . . . . "

7. Give students index cards to write down any questions they might be too embarrassed to verbalize.

■ *Summary:*

Each student completes the following sentence: Today I learned . . . .

Note: Using index-card questions, modify future lesson plans as needed. You may want to address a few of these questions during each session, and allow several more opportunities for students to write anonymous questions.

■ *Materials:*

Get Acquainted sheets
3×5 index cards
pencils
grapes
bowl

Dear Parent:

Your daughter, _____ , has expressed an interest in being involved in a pregnancy education/support group.

The group will meet once a week and will allow your child to meet with other pregnant teens. The group will be led by a trained counselor who is skilled in promoting a safe atmosphere for communication. The basic ground rule is strict confidentiality.

Students involved in the group will miss class once a week (during a different class period each week) and have agreed to make arrangements in advance to remain current in their class work.

If you would like futher information on this group please feel free to contact me

at _____ .

Counselor

_____

Please sign below if you agree to allow your child to participate in this group.

_____

Name _____ Date _____

Get Acquainted Exercise

Directions: Answer the following questions and then share the information with your partner.

1. What is your name? Are you the oldest, middle, youngest, or only child in your family?

2. Who are you most like in your family? Why?

3. Who do you think loves you most in the world? (can be more than one person)

4. What do you enjoy doing in your spare time?

5. What do you like best about yourself?

6. If you could change one thing about yourself, what would it be and why?

7. Where do you think you'll be in 5 years and what do you think you'll be doing?

8. Whom are you depending on most right now?

Session 2: Pregnancy Group

■ *Icebreaker:*

Students will each reach into a bag and select a hard-boiled "egg baby." If it has a blue dot, it's a boy, if it has a pink dot, it's a girl. Allow students to draw faces on their babies and ask them to talk about what they think their baby will look like.

■ *Review:*

In the last session students learned each other's names and a little about each other. Have each student recall something she remembers about a member of the group.

■ *Skill-Building or Awareness Activity:*

1. After students have finished decorating their egg babies, explain the rules for the egg-baby assignments.

   a. Students must keep their eggs with them at all times, or they must hire a responsible babysitter.

   b. Students must keep a realistic diary of feeding, diaper changes, and hours of sleep.

   c. They will report back to the group in a week.

2. Hand out the pregnancy quiz and allow time for students to complete it.

3. Discuss correct/incorrect answers and clear up any misconceptions.

4. Ask if there is anything else they would like to discuss.

5. End with the open-ended statement, What I liked most/least about this session was . . . .

■ *Summary:*

Students complete the following: Today I was surprised that . . . .

Note: Evaluate students' reality level by listening to how they describe what their babies will look like in the future.

■ *Materials:*

Hard-boiled eggs—half with pink dots, half with blue
magic markers
small wicker baskets to carry eggs in
pregnancy quiz

Pregnancy Quiz

Put a T on the line if the statement is true, an F if the statement is false.

_____ 1. A woman must eat carefully to supply adequate protein, carbohydrates, and fat to the fetus.

_____ 2. A woman can safely diet during pregnancy.

_____ 3. Common discomforts of pregnancy include nausea, constipation, heartburn.

_____ 4. It is okay to use drugs or alcohol during pregnancy as long as it is in moderation.

_____ 5. You should stop exercising when you find out you are pregnant.

_____ 6. The first three months of pregnancy are least important, so you may continue old habits without care.

_____ 7. During the first three months of pregnancy the mother will probably have extra energy.

_____ 8. Prenatal vitamins guarantees that the mother receives needed nutrients.

_____ 9. Because you are a teen, you have no rights concerning your health care.

_____ 10. Smoking is not harmful to the developing baby.

Pregnancy Quiz Answers

1. T

2. F Pregnancy is not a time to diet. The developing baby needs nutrients to grow.

3. T

4. F Anything you feel the effects of, the baby can feel the effects of. It is dangerous to use drugs or alcohol.

5. F You should consult your doctor before continuing your regular exercise program, but exercise is a good habit that usually can be continued during pregnancy.

6. F In many ways the first three months are most important. Bad habits should be corrected.

7. F Most women report that they feel tired more during the first three months than they do throughout the rest of the pregnancy.

8. T

9. F Do not feel intimidated by doctors or nurses. Ask.

10. F Smoking during pregnancy can reduce oxygen to the developing fetus and can result in low birth weight.

Session 3: Pregnancy Group

■ *Icebreaker:*

Each student in the circle will briefly tell the group about her last doctor's appointment and what she learned.

■ *Skill-Building or Awareness Activity:*

1. Moving around the circle, have each student report on her egg-baby experience.

2. Discuss with them the differences between this activity and real life. (Pregnant teens are often unaware of the realities of having a baby. They imagine a dream-like existence after the baby is born. Your goal as group leader is to help them understand the reality of having a baby.)

3. Using the Personal Issues handout, ask the questions one at a time and allow them time to answer.

4. End with a summary of the discussion and, if necessary, what question the group will begin with next week.

■ *Summary:*

Students complete the sentence, Today I learned . . . .

Note: This lesson plan may be used for two sessions if trust level is high and students do not get through all the questions. Modify future lesson plans accordingly.

■ *Materials:*

Personal Issues handout
Pencils

Name _____ Date _____

Personal Issues

Be prepared to discuss the following questions with the group.

1. Do you have any definite plans for after the birth of the baby?

2. How has your relationship with the father of the baby changed since you found out you were pregnant?

3. How did your parents react when you told them you were pregnant, and how has your relationship with them changed since you told them?

4. Have you lost any friends because you are pregnant? Have your friends supported your decisions concerning this pregnancy?

5. Do you see yourself any differently than before you become pregnant?

6. Are you planning on staying in school? If yes, how will you manage school and baby? If no, what will you be doing instead?

7. Are you receiving regular prenatal care, and with whom?

8. What are you most afraid of concerning this pregnancy?

9. How do you think having a baby will change your life?

10. If you could change one thing in your life right now, other than being pregnant, what would it be?

Session 4: Pregnancy Group

■ *Icebreaker:*

Using any relaxation tape or relaxation exercise, have students learn the value of relaxation. Remind them that this will be useful when they go into labor.

■ *Review:*

Have students talk about something they learned from the last session.

■ *Skill-Building or Awareness Activity:*

1. A guest speaker from a hospital, clinic, or birthing center will show pictures of the fetus and the stages of labor and delivery and will explain them. She will also tell students about the kinds of painkillers that are available and their effects.

2. Students will ask the speaker questions. (Students may have so many questions that you may want to lengthen the session or have one speaker to discuss the developing fetus and one to discuss the labor process.)

■ *Summary:*

Each student completes the following: Today I was surprised about . . . .

Note: Guest speakers from Lamaze or Better Birth Foundation. They will bring teaching aides.

■ *Materials:*

3×5 index cards

Session 5: Pregnancy Group

■ *Icebreaker:*

Play a round of "telephone." Make up a story about yourself and include details. Have students whisper the message from one to another, and have the last student tell the message to the group. The message has usually been altered. Explain to the students that listening to "others" rather than the actual source of information is usually the reason for misconceptions. That is why you are providing them with the source of information: teen mothers who will tell them about their experiences.

■ *Skill-Building or Awareness Activity:*

1. Remind students of the values rule and confidentiality rule.

2. Ask each mother to tell her story, including the decision-making processes that she went through. Ask that they include how they feel about those decisions now. Also ask those who kept their babies to talk about their responsibilities and how they manage school, or to share their feelings about dropping out if that was their choice.

3. Allow students time to ask questions.

■ *Summary:*

Students complete the sentence, Today I learned . . . .

Note: If students don't have enough time to answer/ask all the questions that they need to, you may ask them if they feel comfortable giving each other their phone numbers.

■ *Materials:*

Two or three teen mothers (don't get them all from your school)
A teen mother who had to drop out of school
A teen who gave her baby up for adoption

Session 6: Pregnancy Group

■ *Icebreaker:*

Hand each student strips of paper with every group member's name on it. Have each write a message or wish to each girl. Collect all the messages and sort them by name, then give each group member an envelope of wishes.

■ *Skill-Building or Awareness Activity:*

1. Remind students that because it is the last session they can deal with new material on an individual basis with the counselor.

2. Ask if there are any unresolved issues that should be dealt with before the group ends.

3. Allow students to share feelings about the group's end.

4. Have students complete group evaluation.

5. Make arrangements with individuals to meet their specific needs.

Note: Use the results of the evaluations to modify future groups.

■ *Materials:*

Envelopes
Strips of paper with each group member's name on it. Make enough so that student has a strip with every other group member's name on it.
Group evaluation

Dear:

Dear:

Dear:

Dear:

Dear:

Dear:

Group Counseling for School Counselors

Pregnancy Group Evaluation

Please answer these questions as honestly as possible. Your answers will help us to modify future groups.

1. Was the group what you expected it to be?

2. Did you receive all the information you needed from group sessions? If not, what should be added?

3. Would you prefer to meet individually with your counselor to discuss your situation, or do you prefer group sessions?

4. Which group sessions were most helpful?

5. Which sessions were least helpful and why?

6. What can you suggest that would improve the group experience?

7. Do you feel that pregnancy support/education groups should be offered to pregnant teens in the future?

8. On a scale of 1 to 10, 10 being the best, how would you rate the overall group experience?

   1   2   3   4   5   6   7   8   9   10

New-Student Programs

Grade Level: Upper Elementary, Middle School, High School	
Time Required: Two Sessions	
Authors: Greg Brigman, Barbara Earley	

There are many ways counselors can help facilitate a new student's adjustment to moving and getting started in a new school. We have developed a program that combines a small group meeting led by trained peer helpers, a peer buddy system and a classroom buddy. We have included an additional group lesson plan that we have used as an extension of the new-student group for new students who requested more group time.

The small group meeting lesson plan and the extension plan follow the explanation of the peer helper system and classroom buddy plan.

■ *Peer Helper System*

Trained peer helpers lead small group meetings to welcome new students. Approximately 4–6 weeks after this meeting (usually just after report cards), the peer helpers that led the group sessions meet individually with each group member. Each peer helper completes the following structured outline as he/she discusses how things are going for the new student.

New Student _____ Date _____

1. How are your grades? You have received a report card by now.

   Math _____ Science _____ Social Studies _____ Lang Arts _____

   Elective _____ Elective_____
   Rate how satisfied you are with your grades on a 1–10 scale, 1 meaning not at all
   satisfied and 10 meaning very satisfied _____ .

   If student rates satisfaction with grades at below 7, ask if he/she would like to
   have a peer tutor. Explain peer tutoring. Yes _____ No _____

   What subject? _____

2. How are things going with you and your teachers? 1–10 _____

   If not satisfactory to student, peer helper helps student explore what could be
   done to improve relations with the teacher. Peer asks, "Would you like to talk
   with a counselor about getting along with your teachers?"

   Yes _____ No _____ Explain who the counselors are and how to see them.

3. How satisfied are you with making friends here? 1–10 _____

   If student is not satisfied, peer helper listens, explores the student's problem,
   discusses what activities the student is involved in or might like to try. Talk about
   other activities in and out of school that are available.

4. Peer helper summarizes meeting and tells new student about next meeting in 6
   weeks and any follow-up before then. Example: "One of the counselors will get
   in touch with you regarding peer tutoring, or to discuss how things are going
   with teachers and friends."

   Throughout this meeting the peer helper is using the listening and other communication skills taught in peer helper training. The goal is to have a warm, personal meeting and to give some positive life to the above structured outline.

Classroom Buddy Plan

The classroom buddy system is a plan to help new students feel more comfortable and become better acquainted with our school. Each classroom teacher selects two students (one male, one female) who agree to be classroom buddies.

The following is a lesson plan for a training session for classroom buddies.

■ *PBS—Phantom Buddy System: Introductory Meeting* ("The Phantom" is our school mascot; any name can be used.)

I. Introduce counselors, administrator, registration and testing personnel.

II. Congratulations on being chosen as a buddy or thank you for volunteering. Being a buddy to new students shows your care and concern about others and that you want them to feel a part of this school.

III. Questions
- How many of you remember being a new student?
- What did you think on the first day?
- How were you treated?
- How long before you felt comfortable here?
- What do we do in our classes when a new student walks in?
- What were some things you worried about before coming to school the first day?
      what students would wear
      would I make friends
      would I like my teachers
      would I get lost
      would I be afraid
      would I be able to open my locker

   Discuss these items and have the partners offer suggestions. Talk with the buddies about how new students sometimes act aloof. Why do you think they might appear that way? (Because they are frightened and are trying to look as though they're comfortable.)

IV. Role of the Buddy

   Since this is the beginning of the school year we have about 100 new students who have registered during the summer and the first week of school. We'll give you a list of those students so you can meet them and talk with them. As new students come in during the year, you can meet with them on the first day and help them find everything.

   You have a list of suggested activities that might be helpful to a new student. Please get a partner, the person seated next to you, and come up with some ideas for each of these suggestions. I'll give 10 minutes, and at the end of that time we'll share our ideas with the whole group.

V. Other Services for New Students
  ● Peer helpers' new-student group
  ● Peer helpers talking individually with new students
  ● Referral to counselors if new students are not adjusting to school
  ● Counselors talk to parents and teachers of new students
  ● Friendship groups by the counselors
  ● Coupon book that they can redeem for items such as bookmarks from librarians or cookies from the cafeteria

The responsibility for helping new students is not yours alone. Enlist the help of your friends, help students get involved in clubs and activities, and let them know what is offered in the community.

You have an important job and are providing a much needed service for new students. We'll be in touch with you throughout the year to see how things are going. If you see that a new student is having a difficult time at school or at home, we would like for you to let one of the counselors know.

Name _____ Date _____

Phantom Buddy Suggested Activities

1. Sit next to new students in class (for the first week).

2. Help with locker combinations (demonstrate).

3. Take them to class or match them with a student who is going to their class.

4. Find out their interests and introduce them to others who share the interest(s).

5. Include them with your friends at lunch.

6. Give the new students a phone call to check on how things are going (after first and second week). Ask how you can be helpful.

7. Inform the students of activities after school and in the community in which they may have an interest.

8. Tell students about who is available to help new students (e.g., peer tutors, counselors, teachers).

Group Counseling for School Counselors

TO: HOMEROOM TEACHERS

FROM: COUNSELORS

RE: PHANTOM BUDDY SYSTEM—PBS

To help our new students feel more comfortable and become better acquainted with our school, we would like to begin a Phantom Buddy System.

Most of you already have a procedure for helping new students. We want to extend that program with some specific activities, phone calls, notes, and being in touch. We'll also have peer helpers working with new students in a group and then individually.

Please select a boy and a girl to be buddies for your homeroom. Please choose students who are open, caring, and who want to be a buddy.

We will meet with them and go over this list of duties. You might want to read them this list.

PHANTOM BUDDY ROLE: (Some suggested activities)

1. Sit next to new students in class (for first week).
2. Help with locker combinations.
3. Take them to class or match them with a student who is going to their class.
4. Include them with your friends at lunch.
5. Phone—call once per week for first 2–3 weeks.
6. Share some activities after school (how to join).
7. Tell students where they can get extra help (i.e., peer tutoring, counselors, teachers).

Please turn in two names to one of the counselors by _____ .

We will meet with these students on _____ during period _____ .

— —

HOMEROOM TEACHER _____

PHANTOM BUDDY SYSTEM

NAME _____

NAME _____

                   Group Counseling for School Counselors

Session 1: New Student Group

NOTE: These are the lesson plans conducted by trained peer helpers working in pairs as described on page 245.

■ *Introduction:*

Introduce self, go over purpose of group, and go around group—members say names.

■ *Icebreaker:*

1. Students in pairs interview each other, then introduce partner to group. The following information is used for introductions:

   - where moving from

   - brothers, sisters

   - hobbies, interests

   - pets

2. After each introduction, group leader asks person introduced if anything was left out. Thank person doing introduction.

3. Discuss with group:

   - What were some things you noticed people had in common?

   - What were some things you noticed that were different?

   - Who came from the farthest away, closest?

■ *Skill-Building or Awareness Activity:*

1. Discuss with group:

   - How many have moved more than once?

   - What are some fun things about moving?

   - What are some things about moving that you don't like?

   When leader gets answers to the above, ask: How many of you have felt that way, or agree with that? When did you feel that way?

   - How have you found the people here?

   - How many have found at least one friend already?

   - What are some ways you go about making new friends? (Spend some time on this question)

   - What are some things about this school that are like your old school?

   - How long do you think it usually takes to get used to a new school, to feel comfortable?

- What are some things people can do to help you feel comfortable here?
- What's one thing you like about this school? (Give them a moment to think, then go around the circle for responses.)

2. Getting Involved

   Students who have been new in the past tell us that getting involved in activities with other students helps them feel connected and is helpful in fitting in.

   - What are some activities that are available for you to join?

   After group brainstorms activities and how to join, each leader shares list, pointing out any not mentioned.

3. Knowledge About School

   - Do you all know who the principal is?
   - Do you all know the school's colors and mascot?
   - How many know where the clinic is?
   - If you lose something, do you know where lost-and-found is?
   - Have you met any of the counselors here? Their names are _____ . They can be helpful if you need to talk individually. They offer groups and come to classrooms. Peer tutoring is also available.

■ *Summary:*

Think about one thing you've learned about this school today—we'll go around and share.

I enjoyed meeting you today and look forward to seeing you again. Each of you will have a peer helper buddy who will check with you in a couple of weeks to see how things are going.

Session 2: New-Student Group

■ *Introduction:*

Go around circle and say names.

■ *Icebreaker:*

1. Introduce topic: Today we'll be talking about friendship. Most people moving into a new place are anxious to make new friends. How many of you feel that way?

2. Voting Activity
Let's take a look at how you think and feel about friends. We'll start with a voting activity—raise your hand if you agree.

> How many of you . . .
> have a best friend?
> have a good friend of the opposite sex?
> have had an argument with a good friend lately?
> have a friend that you can talk to about your problems?
> have ever had a day when you felt as if you didn't have any friends?
> think a friend is someone who will do whatever you say?
> think a friend should always agree with you?
> have a brother or sister who is also your friend?

■ *Skill-Building or Awareness Activity:*

1. Complete "Making Friends" sheet (page 52).
Divide group into pairs to share answers. Then share answers with big group.

2. We've talked about making friends. Now let's look at what kind of people we like as friends.
As a group, have students suggest 10 qualities a friend should have. Leader may ask quiet member to record. After 10 qualities are listed, vote on top two qualities. Record votes. Leader comments on what's most important to group.

3. Ask group to silently consider whether or not they have these qualities themselves.

■ *Summary:*

Each member responds to: Today I learned . . . . Remind group of any scheduled follow-up.

Resources for New Students

Greenwald, Dorothy. *Coping With Moving*. Rosen Publishing Group, New York, 1987.

Lane, Kenneth E., and Ted Dickey. "New Students and Grief." *The School Counselor Vol. 35, May 1988*. This article incorporates Kubler-Ross's stages of grief in working with new students.

A New Child in School, a brochure mainly for parents but also for school personnel. Can be obtained from Boys Town Communications and Public Service Division, Boys Town, NE 68010.

PERSONAL GROWTH FOR TEACHERS

Personal Growth for Teachers

Time Required: Nine Sessions	
Authors: Barbara Earley, Greg Brigman	

■ *How This Group Developed*

Because teachers frequently experience stress and burnout, we decided to offer an after-school personal-growth group. Offering the group shows teachers your concern for their well-being, which is appreciated. Working with adults is rewarding for the counselor and gives teachers opportunities to share ideas. Serving refreshments and modeling a relaxed atmosphere is in itself therapeutic. It is certainly an excellent way to get to know each other.

Several Methods for Quick and Easy
Teacher Groups

If you feel hesitant or uncertain about offering groups for teachers, your first experience could be to have speakers for each session. You might begin by offering an activity once a month or having four sessions offered weekly. There could be four speakers on one topic such as stress, or a different topic each time. Consult your local mental health agency, hospital speakers' bureau, a private therapist, or ask another school counselor. Your responsibilities would include: conducting an icebreaker with the group; discussing objectives; introducing the speaker; leading a discussion after the speaker; and concluding with a summary and written evaluation.

Another idea is to offer a series of video- or audiotapes based on a particular topic of interest to the participants. You may wish to use the "Love" tapes by Leo Buscaglia, or a series of relaxation tapes.

As you begin to feel more comfortable leading groups, you could offer a staff-development course such as *STET (Systematic Training for Effective Teaching)*. If time does not allow for a fifty-hour course, you could do small segments on topics such as encouragement or the democratic classroom.

An easy and ready-for-use group lesson plan is the *Encouragement Book* by Don Dinkmeyer. The activities in this book are great for motivating participants to be more loving, motivating, respectful, and encouraging to themselves and others.

Cover a chapter per week. If you obtain copies for each participant, you can begin with a discussion of the reading. Next, lead the group through the chapter's activities. If participants do not have copies, the leader summarizes the key points before and/or after the activities.

A good standard format for group sessions is:
    Icebreaker
    Review of Last Session
    Discussion and Activity
    Summary

Personal Growth for Teachers

■ *Group Objectives:*

    To get to know other faculty members better
    To learn about yourself
    To develop personal growth goals and plans

■ *Time:*

    7 one-hour meetings after school

■ *Group Composition:*

    Faculty members

■ *Group Rules:*

Rules for adult groups are similar to rules for student groups. The rules need to come from the participants and should include confidentiality, right to pass or not participate, and respect of others' opinions (no put-downs).

Session 1: Personal Growth

■ *Introduction and Overview:*

1. Introduce the group by outlining its purpose. Example: "We'll be meeting for the next 8 weeks from 3–4 p.m. During this time I hope you'll become more aware of your strengths and look for some areas that you may want to enhance. Our meeting together in a personal-growth group indicates that we are healthy individuals who have high expectations about the quality of life. We all have times of stress and disappointments. We also have goals that we may not pursue because of our busy lives. The group time will provide an opportunity for you to look more closely at yourself and those goals. Meeting together each week will help us get to know each other in a personal and non-threatening manner. You will decide how open you want to be with the group. A feeling of trust will help us be more open with each other. The trust will develop as we come to feel that group members will keep what we say here confidential."

2. Establish—as a group—some group rules. Members will come up with the same rules that students do: confidentiality, respect for each other, and no put-downs. (Members should all agree on the rules.)

3. Housekeeping: Group members may take turns bringing refreshments. Encourage them to be on time.

4. Explain the purpose and advantages of keeping a journal. Example: "It is helpful to keep a journal while you are in the group. You will have opportunities to write down your thoughts while we are doing an activity and to write an 'I learned' statement at the end of each session. During the week, as you work on an assignment or have thought about the group, writing in the journal will help bring focus to your ideas.

■ *Icebreaker: Name Tag Activity*

Sample Name Tag

Place where you spent 5 days of bliss	Something you have planned that you are looking forward to
	Name
Most serene, peaceful place in home	List places you have lived

Members are given a 5″ x 8″ index card to write information. (See previous page for a sample name tag.) The leader gives directions for each corner of the card. When the group has finished, each person gets with a partner and shares what he/she has written. Have the group spend some time with the details. For example, in the corner that asks "list places you have lived," have participants choose the one that meant most to them. Perhaps it was the place where the most growth occurred, a happy place, or a place where there was a crisis.

Back in the big group, have group members share an "I learned . . . " statement.

■ *Skill-Building or Awareness Activity:*

"What Are You Doing for the Rest of Your Life?"

1. Group members list 20 things they would like to do that they haven't done yet in their lives. Allow 10–15 minutes for them to list the activities. In the spaces after listing the activities, make a mark indicating:

   - one you can begin right away

   - one you would like to begin in 5 years

   - how many require money

   - which ones you would have chosen 5 years ago

   The additional spaces can be used if you have time, and might include topics such as:

   - which ones you prefer doing alone

   - which ones you prefer doing with people

   - which ones a spouse or significant other would choose

   - which ones require additional training and education

2. Ask participants to share some of the categories with a partner or with the larger group.

3. Ask the group to share aloud.
   Who had one that was about:
   > travel
   > profession/career
   > relationships
   > physical
   > spiritual
   > intellectual

■ *Summary:*

1. Ask participants to complete these sentences in their journals:
   > I learned . . . .
   > I was surprised that . . . .
   > One activity I want to start right away . . . .

   Share them with the group.

2. Put on music (soft, instrumental) for 60 seconds: Ask participants to picture themselves doing that one thing that they want to begin right away.

■ *Assignment:*

Share your 20 things with a spouse or significant other, or spend time thinking about how to begin on this new task.

What Are You Doing for the Rest of Your Life?

List in the column below 20 things that you would like to do, experience, achieve, try, or enjoy before you die.

1.										
2.										
3.										
4.										
5.										
6.										
7.										
8.										
9.										
10.										
11.										
12.										
13.										
14.										
15.										
16.										
17.										
18.										
19.										
20.										

What did you find out about yourself? I learned that _____

_____

I was surprised (or pleased) that _____

_____

Session 2: Personal Growth

Alfred Adler believed that our primary goal in life was to feel a sense of belonging. Adler stated that there were three tasks in life: work, friends, and intimate relationships. Most of us have an imbalance among these three areas. Nobody is perfect. One way of checking our satisfaction with our lives is to look at these three areas. Then we need to decide which area needs the most attention right now.

■ *Icebreaker:*

My name is . . . and the high point of my week was . . . .

■ *Skill-Building or Awareness Activity:*

A feeling of connectedness is essential for self-esteem. To be happy, we have to feel that we belong. Our connectedness network includes our family, friends, and co-workers.

1. The leader asks the following four questions, one at a time. After each question, ask participants to write a brief impression in their journals. After approximately one minute for writing, ask for volunteers to share. This sharing should not be a go-round. There should be no pressure to share.

   - How do you feel connected to your family of origin? Close your eyes and picture yourself approaching the family at a reunion. Are you welcomed with open arms and positive comments, or do you anticipate cutting remarks and disapproval?

   - How does it feel walking up to your front door at the end of the day?

   - What do your friends mean to you? Do you have friends for confidantes, for fun, and as models?

   - How do you relate to your co-workers? If you were out of work for three days, would you be missed?

2. Connectedness handout. Explain one category at a time and have the group list people for each area.

   For example:

   - *Confidantes* are those people you can really trust with your intimate feelings and thoughts, those with whom you can share joys and sorrows.

   - *Intellectual Stretchers* are people with whom you philosophize, those who expand your knowledge and your creative thinking.

   - *Health* people are those who hand you your running shoes, who inspire and encourage your taking care of yourself.

   - *Fun and Adventure* people enjoy life, try new things, and encourage you to take part.

- *Spiritual* has to do with those people in your life who cause you to examine and expand your beliefs and thoughts.

- *Chicken Soup* people are those who would visit you if you were sick and bring you chicken soup. These are the people who are always there to help you out.

- *Mentors/Guides* are people you want to learn from. They have talents and skills that they want to share with you.

Summary:

I learned . . . .
I relearned . . . .
I can see that I need to . . . .

Name _____ Date _____

My Connectedness Network

Family	Friends	Co-Workers and Others
CONFIDANTES		
INTELLECTUAL STRETCHERS		
HEALTH		
FUN AND ADVENTURE		
SPIRITUAL		
CHICKEN SOUP		
MENTORS/GUIDES		

Group Counseling for School Counselors

Session 3: Personal Growth

■ *Icebreaker:*

1. Today I'm a . . . on a 1–10 scale, and one thing I'm looking forward to in the next week is . . . .

2. Review last session.

■ *Skill-Building or Awareness Activity:*

1. Connectedness handout, continued. Usually this activity requires time this session for completion (see last session).

2. Identifying Connections handout: Ask group members to take a few minutes to complete this sheet. After completing, have participants get into groups of three to share the responses to each. Remind the group that everyone has the right to pass on any part of the handout.

■ *Summary:*

Ask group to return to larger circle and share how it felt to complete the Connectedness sheet and the Identifying Connections sheet.

Name ———————————————————————— Date ————————————————

Identifying Connections

Four people who love you

———————————————————————   ————————————————————————

———————————————————————   ————————————————————————

Three people you have learned a lot from

———————————————————————

———————————————————————

———————————————————————

Three people who have learned something from you

———————————————————————

———————————————————————

———————————————————————

Four people who usually smile at you

———————————————————————   ————————————————————————

———————————————————————   ————————————————————————

Two people who have helped you in an important way

———————————————————————

———————————————————————

Three people who are usually kind to you

———————————————————————

———————————————————————

———————————————————————

Session 4: Personal Growth

■ *Icebreaker:*

1. One quality about myself that I'm proud of is . . . .

2. Review last week's meeting.

■ *Skill-Building or Awareness Activity:*

Relaxation Training

1. Introduce the importance of learning to deeply relax. Mention regular practice, how images are helpful, and how relaxation creates your inner sanctuary.

   Many relaxation techniques are readily available. Two of the most popular include: *The Relaxation Response*—Herbert Benson, *Progressive Relaxation*—Edmund Jacobson.

   There are also many useful cassette tapes that incorporate relaxation training and positive imagery—some with helpful ideas on avoiding self-defeating behavior and improving self-esteem. You may want to guide the relaxation with or without imagery.

   For this session we frequently use the *Taking Control of Your Life* cassette tape listed below.

2. Ask the participants to listen for 2–3 important ideas and be ready to discuss their choices after the tape. After going through the tape, ask who was able to deeply relax to see clearly the images described.

   Ask each person to identify his/her favorite image. Then, one by one, share 1–3 important ideas from the tape.

■ *Summary:*

Ask group members to complete one of the following: One thing I learned or relearned today was . . . . Something that surprised me was . . . .

■ *Materials:*

Taking Control of Your Life, Robert Griswold, Effective Learning Systems, Inc., Edina, Minnesota.

Session 5: Personal Growth

■ *Icebreaker:*

1. One thing I could teach someone else is . . . (non-school related).

2. Review last meeting.

■ *Skill-Building or Awareness Activity:*

"Irrational Beliefs" Handout

1. Ask the participants to read the 11 irrational beliefs by Albert Ellis and choose the 2–3 that cause them the most trouble, or that they can't see anything wrong with, or that influence their life the most.

2. In groups of 3–4, ask members to share the above. For irrational beliefs that seem appropriate to some, the other group members provide reasons why the belief is irrational or can cause problems. Designate a spokesperson to give a summary of small group to large group. Ask the small groups to report back a summary of their discussion.

3. If time permits, the leader can give a brief overview of Ellis's ABC model. See any of the numerous books by Ellis on R.E.T. (Rational Emotive Therapy).

■ *Summary:*

Ask participants to record a summary of key points and their feelings about the meeting in their journal. Ask for volunteers to share their entries with the group.

Irrational Beliefs

It is essential that one be loved or approved of by virtually everyone in his community.

One must be perfectly competent, adequate, and achieving to consider oneself worthwhile.

Some people are bad, wicked, or villainous, and therefore should be blamed and punished.

It is a terrible catastrophe when things are not as one wants them to be.

Unhappiness is caused by outside circumstances, and the individual has no control over it.

Dangerous or fearsome things are causes for great concern, and their possibility must be continually dwelt upon.

It is easier to avoid certain difficulties and self-responsibilities than to face them.

One should be dependent on others and must have someone stronger on whom to rely.

Past experiences and events are the determiners of present behavior; the influence of the past cannot be eradicated.

One should be quite upset over other people's problems and disturbances.

There is always a right or perfect solution to every problem and it must be found or the results will be catastrophic.

* * *

". . . people do not *get upset* but instead *upset themselves* by insisting that (a) they should be outstandingly loved and accomplished, (b) other people should be incredibly fair and giving, and (c) the world should be exceptionally easy and munificent." Albert Ellis, 1973.

Group Counseling for School Counselors

Session 6: Personal Growth

■ *Icebreaker:*

1. What three things do you want for your children? or students in your class? or young people today?

2. Review Session 5 and ask:

   • Who has done something about an item on his/her list of 20 things?

   • Who has set up some times to get together with some of their important connection people?

   • Who has tried any relaxation techniques?

   • Who has caught himself or herself with any irrational ideas?

■ *Skill-Building or Awareness Activity:*

1. Guided Imagery: "Enjoying Your Life" (to be read to the group).

2. "Picturing Your Ideal Self" (also to be read to the group). Write a plan for reaching your ideal self in 5 years.

■ *Summary:*

Each participant completes the following and shares with group: One thing I learned today was . . . .

Enjoying Your Life

Developing your skills in relaxation and imagery is extremely beneficial in your quest to get more joy and satisfaction from your life. Now we will go through a series of five imagery exercises, each lasting from 15 seconds to 2 minutes. Following this series, we will use our imagination to look at our "ideal self" and develop a five-year plan for approaching our image. You will have an opportunity to share part of your plan in groups of three. Let's begin.

Take several slow, deep breaths, get into a comfortable position, and close your eyes as we practice using our imagination.

1. Picture yourself in your favorite chair. See the color, feel the texture and comfortable feelings you have when you sit there. (pause 15–20 seconds)

2. Picture an ideal place—a place where you feel tranquil, serene and balanced. This can be a place you've been or a place you create in your imagination. (pause 30–60 seconds)

3. Picture a fun experience you've had recently. (pause 30 seconds)

4. Picture a beautiful sunrise—see the pinks, blues, clouds—feel the wind, hear the birds. (pause 30 seconds)

5. Picture yourself on the beach alone. Watch the waves, listen to the rhythm, feel the warmth of the sand. As you inhale, imagine the incoming waves bringing you energy, peace, happiness; and as you exhale, imagine the receding waves taking away your worries, concerns, stress. (pause 2–3 minutes)

Leader uses "Picturing Your Ideal Self" sheet to continue this activity.

Picturing Your Ideal Self

Picture yourself as already having all the positive qualities or traits you believe are important. This is your ideal self. Don't hold back—see yourself just as you want to be. Feel the gracefulness of your movement—the poise and balance. Feel the confidence, the courage you have to be yourself, to say and do what you feel and think even if others disapprove, because you know that happiness is the absence of self-hate and approval seeking. Feel yourself relaxed and at ease, alert and aware, with tremendous energy. See yourself taking action on the things that are important in your life.

Feel the contentment of knowing you do whatever it takes to take good care of yourself, because you know that without good self-care, there won't be anything to share with others. Deeply relax and allow these positive feelings to soak in.

In a moment I will ask you to write out a plan for reaching this state within the next five years. Picture what steps are needed. Break your plan into easy-to-achieve chunks. Set a time to begin one small part. Don't overload—trying too much at once is a key to discouragement. (pause 2–3 minutes)

In just a moment I'll ask you to open your eyes. (pause 10–15 seconds)

Now slowly open your eyes and slowly move around and stretch in your chair. Take a moment to write yourself some note on your plan. In groups of three, share your plans (allow enough time for everyone to share). Now complete your plan write-up. Be specific, clear, and realistic.

Session 7: Personal Growth

■ *Icebreaker:*

1. Rate how you're feeling on a scale of 1–10, and share one thing you've done to nurture yourself lately.

2. Review last meeting.

■ *Skill-Building or Awareness Activity:*

Participants get into groups according to birth order—oldest child, middle child, youngest child, and only child. Each group lists the characteristics of that position and how it felt to grow up in that position.

Each group has a recorder, who reports the characteristics to the whole group. One way to accomplish this reporting is to have each group list their characteristics on a poster or blackboard. After all groups have reported, the lists should be side by side for easy comparison. The discussion can evolve into how these positions carry over into adult life and how these characteristics are seen in participants' own children.

Sometimes participants may not feel that they fit neatly into a profile of only, youngest, oldest, or middle child. Refer to your readings of Adlerian psychology, which explains that it may be your *perception* of your position in the family, rather than the actual birth order that influences behavior. Example: Ask a sibling or parent how they saw you, and you may get a different perception from yours. The psychological birth order, may be more significant than the physical birth order. For instance, the second child may exhibit characteristics of the oldest child.

■ *Summary:*

Ask participants to complete one of the following:

One thing I learned was . . . .

One thing I relearned was . . . .

One thing that surprised me was . . . .

The idea that birth order affects our personality development is an Adlerian concept. For additional information, you may want to read:
STET (Systematic Training for Effective Teaching) by Don Dinkmeyer
Adlerian Family Counseling by Oscar Christenson

Session 8: Personal Growth

Note: This activity was expanded to meet the needs of principals, teachers, and parents by Mary Joe Hannaford, who has specialized in group counseling and leadership seminars.

■ *Icebreaker:*

1. Describe your favorite teacher. What qualities did you appreciate most?

2. Review last week's session.

■ *Skill-Building or Awareness Activity:*

Attitudes Toward Authority

1. Introduction to activity. This activity is based on transactional analysis. TA was developed by Eric Berne and popularized by the writings of Tom Harris (*I'm OK, You're OK*), Jongeward, James, and the Gouldings. "TA is an interactional therapy grounded on the assumption that we make current decisions based on past premises that were once appropriate to our survival needs but may no longer be valid." TA stresses that people can change and make new decisions that do not necessarily adhere to the rules and regulations they learned as children. (*Theory and Practice of Group Counseling,* Gerald Corey, page 311.)

2. Directions: Draw a T square on a piece of paper. (Demonstrate on the chalkboard or a flipchart how you want this to be done.) On the top of the T square, write the name of the most powerful authority figure in your life before age 10. You must choose one person. If you find it difficult to choose between parents, choose the stronger parent, and then do the exercise again later with the other parent. You may choose a grandparent, or even a neighbor, depending on the makeup of your family. On the left-hand column write a description of that person. On the right-hand column, indicate your responses to that person—your feelings as a child. It is important that you try to look back at the feelings you had then—not the feelings you have now.

3. In the left-hand column, list three positive qualities which you admired in this person. Give some examples. Even if you hated this person, you may find something good if you think about it for a while. Now move to the right-hand column and write your child feelings about those positive qualities. Give some examples. For instance, they may have been so wonderful that you always felt that you couldn't live up, or they have been so terrible that you always felt superior. You may have always felt protected. Get in touch with your feelings.

4. In the left-hand column, list three negative qualities about this person. Give some examples. You may not be able to think of any if you always admired the person. Maybe you thought the person was perfect. That in itself may have been a negative. Now move to the right-hand side and tell how that made you feel as a child.

5. List three adjectives to describe this person. Adjectives might come from the first two descriptions, or they may be a combination of positive and negative. Now move to the right-hand column and describe your child feelings.

6. If you were sick or injured or down emotionally, how would that person have reacted? Give examples—would the person have been loving and nurturing, or would he/she have ignored the crisis and indicated that you must "get on with it"? Now move to the right-hand column and describe your child feelings.

7. What was the message you got as a child about your worth? Was this person telling you that you were important, or that you were in the way? What did you hear, both non-verbally and verbally? Now move to the right-hand column and describe your child feelings.

8. What is the recurring message which you still receive from that person about your worth? It doesn't matter what age the person is now, or even whether that person is still living. You probably still get a message. Now move to the right-hand column and describe your feelings *now*.

9. Take some time to process this information. Look at all of the information which has been brought into your awareness. Share any discoveries you have made about your authority person, your relationship to that person.

   Leader: Allow some silence in order for the processing to begin. Some long-buried memories may have surfaced for some participants. It is possible that someone will discover a happy memory which can be shared with the group. It is not unusual for someone to be touched to the point of tears when reaching back to such memories. Sometimes, for those with a very neglected or harsh childhood, the discovery that they are alone in the group is devastating. Handle these moments gently, without probing deeply.

   Guide the processing with the following questions. Allow members to *volunteer* to participate. Do not have a go-around. You may be touching on ground too tender to confront in a group.

   A. In what way do I express my authority role like the person I just described? What traits do I communicate to others who are my subordinates? children? students?

   B. In what way do I respond to the persons in authority over me in the same way I responded to my childhood authority person?

   C. In view of my past, what are my expectations and needs from people in authority?

   D. In what ways would I like to change the way I express my authority role in relation to my subordinates?

   E. In what ways would I like to change the way I respond to persons in authority over me?

   F. In what ways do I conduct my life according to my childhood "message"?

G. In what ways do I conduct my life in the opposite manner from my "message"?

H. In what way does my present behavior reflect the message?

■ *Summary:*

Complete the following sentences.

From this exercise I have learned . . . .

I have relearned . . . .

I have realized . . . .

I am surprised that . . . .

Note: This activity can elicit very strong emotional responses from participants. Before introducing this activity, be sure you are comfortable with your own authority T-square and with your competence in leading groups of adults. Group members may be told that the activity explores their relationships with their earliest authority figure and that influence on their present authority role. Be sure that they are not pressed to share any feelings. They must know, as in all groups, that it is permissible not to participate.

Name _____ Date _____

My Authority Person	*Child Feeling Response*
1. Three positive qualities . . . _____ _____ _____	Three feelings you had as a child in response to these qualities . . . _____ _____ _____
2. Three negative qualities . . . _____ _____ _____	Three feelings . . . _____ _____ _____
3. Three adjectives . . . _____ _____ _____	Three feelings . . . _____ _____ _____
4. If you were sick . . . _____ _____ _____	Three feelings . . . _____ _____ _____
5. Message about worth . . . _____ _____ _____	Three feelings . . . _____ _____ _____
6. Recurring message . . . _____ _____ _____	Three feelings . . . _____ _____ _____

Group Counseling for School Counselors

Session 9: Personal Growth

■ *Icebreaker:*

One thing I'm looking forward to is . . . .

■ *Closure Activity:*

1. Review of last eight sessions. Ask teachers to recall some of the activities that were meaningful to them and share. After sharing the activities that were most meaningful, ask: What changes can you start right away? Ask participants to write these changes down and then share them with the group. Ask them to identify longer-range changes and what they need to do. After listing these changes, have them share in the group.

2. Pass out strength circles. Ask each teacher to sign his/her name on the strength circle and pass to next teacher. Each teacher writes positive qualities about every other teacher as the strength circles are passed around. These positive comments are written in the outer circle, leaving the inner circle blank.

   After everyone finishes the strength circles, give them back to their owners.

3. We call this next part "Spotlighting" or "Strength Bombardment." One by one the group focuses on a teacher. Each participant tells the focus teacher one or more things that they appreciate about him/her. After everyone has spoken, the next person is spotlighted.

   Note: Instructions for giving and receiving compliments: Direct eye contact. "Mary, one thing I really like about you is . . . ," or, "One thing I appreciate about you is . . . ." The receiver simply smiles and says thank you.

4. To conclude this activity, ask teachers to write in the center of the circle the three most important strengths or positive qualities they see in themselves.

■ *Summary:*

Have participants fill out a group evaluation.

My Strengths

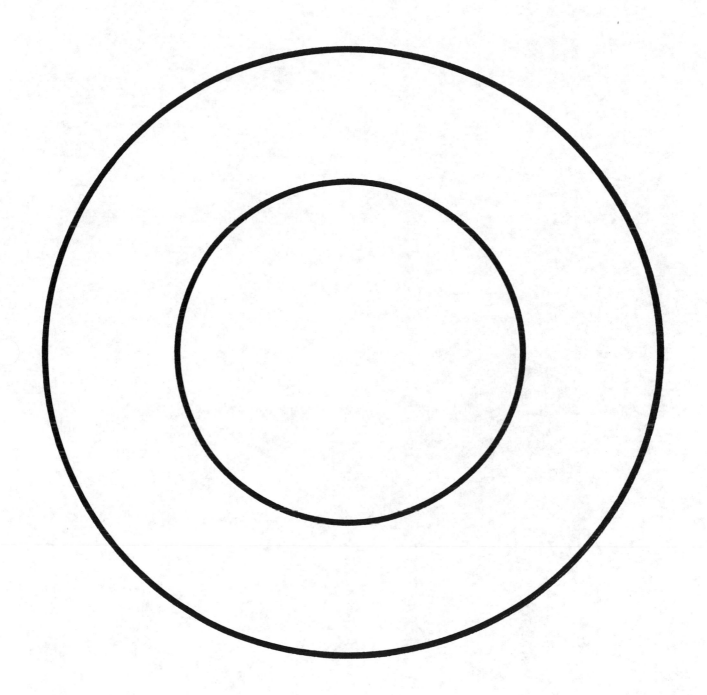

PARENT EDUCATION GROUPS

Parent Education Groups

A comfortable working knowledge of group leadership skills is essential for leading a parent group. Lesson plan format, organization, and group rules are similar to those of student or teacher groups. If you have not led a parent group, you may wish to begin by having speakers while you coordinate the sessions.

Here are suggestions to consider:

- Work with the PTA Family Life Committee and together offer 4 or 6 sessions throughout the year. You might have topics on child abuse, drug prevention, helping your child be successful at school, building self-esteem, or how to manage stress.

- You could lead a discussion group based on a book that members would read, such as *Encouragement* or *Traits of a Healthy Family*.

- Lead a group using materials that are well organized, such as *Systematic Training for Effective Parenting (STEP), STEP/TEEN, Active Parenting,* or *How to Talk So Kids Will Listen.*

- Group for single parents.

- Step-family group.

The effective parent group meets 6–10 sessions for 1½ to 2 hours per session. 10 to 12 parents is a good number. If there are too few parents, it is difficult to have a good discussion. Likewise, too many parents won't permit enough time for everyone to share. An overview or syllabus is effective. The first session should include group rules, purpose, overview, commitment, and assignments. It is important for parents to make the commitment to attend each session. Make an effort to talk with both parents by telephone or in a conference several weeks before the group begins. You can conduct a parent group if only one parent from the family attends, but it is much more productive to have both parents present. If only the mother attends and she is not able to convey her new knowledge and enthusiasm to her husband, there could be more harm than help.

Parents are more likely to attend each session, participate, and belong if they are involved from the beginning. Parents are more committed if they pay for the text and/or the sessions. Payment should be handled by the PTA as a project and should not be received by the leader.

Each session must be interesting, fun, thought-provoking, and hopeful. If participants can feel that there are some answers and some concrete tasks to try, they will become involved and make some changes in their parenting.

Participants can take turns bringing refreshments to enjoy during break or before the session begins. As with other groups, seat parents in a circle for better interaction and eye contact.

Each session should include:

- icebreaker or get-acquainted activity
- review of last session
- discussion of the week's reading assignment
- discussion of their goal or new behavior
- new topic or skill
- summary
- homework assignment

Members should be allowed equal sharing time. Be careful not to permit one member to dominate the session with personal experiences. The reluctant participant may need extra attention and encouragement. These issues can be addressed when the group devises the rules. Remind the group that each person is responsible for his/her behavior and participation in making the group experience a successful one.

Parent groups often get discouraged, play "ain't it awful," and spend too much time discussing how things aren't the way they used to be. It is important for the leader to keep the discussion moving in a positive, helpful direction without too much digression on single topics or family experiences.

Parent group sessions could include these topics:

- encouragement
- self-esteem
- developing responsibility
- communication
- behavior/misbehavior
- understanding
- development stages of the child
- natural and logical consequences
- how to have family meetings

Parent groups are fun, rewarding, hard work, and challenging. Be prepared before you begin and you will enjoy your group.

Resources for Parent Groups

Buntman, Peter, and Saris, Eleanor. *How to Live with Your Teenager.* Birch Tree Press, Pasadena, CA 91107. 1980.

Clemes, Harris, and Bean, Reynold. *How to Teach Children Responsibility. How to Raise Children's Self-Esteem. How to Discipline Children without Feeling Guilty.* I.E.S.S., Inc., P.O. Box 432, Kernersville, NC 27284. 1983.

Curran, Delores. *Traits of a Healthy Family.* Paperbacks for Educators, Washington, MO. 1983.

Dinkmeyer, Don, and Lasoncy, Lewis. *The Encouragement Book.* Prentice-Hall, New Jersey. 1980.

Dinkmeyer, Don, and McKay, Gary. *Systematic Training for Effective Parenting (STEP).* American Guidance Service, Inc., Circle Pines, MN 55014. 1986.

Gould, Shirley. *Teenagers, The Continuing Challenge.* Hawthorn Books, New York. 1977.

Popkin, Michael. *Active Parenting.* Active Parenting, 4669 Roswell Rd., Atlanta, GA 30342 (video-based program). 1987.

Walton, Frank. *Winning Children Over.* Practical Psychology Associates, Chicago, IL 60690. 1980.

Walton, Frank. *Winning Teenagers Over.* Adlerian Child Care books. Order: The Alfred Adler Institute, 618 S. Michigan Ave., Chicago, IL 60605. 1980.

Annotated Bibliography

Bowman, Robert. "Small Group Guidance and Counseling in Schools: A National Survey of School Counselors." *School Counselor*, v34, n4, pp. 256–262, Mar 1987.

Counselors at all levels agreed that small-group counseling is vital and practical.

Buescher, Thomas. "Counseling Gifted Adolescents: A Curriculum Made for Students, Parents and Professionals." *Gifted Child Quarterly*, v31, n2, pp. 90–94, Spr 1987.

A proactive, preventive approach to counseling gifted students is discussed. Key areas include: adolescent growth and development, identity and adjustment, changes in relations, and career paths. A flowchart for implementing the model is included, which is suited for middle or high school.

Coffman, Shirley-Gwinn, and Albert E. Roark. "Likely Candidates for Group Counseling: Adolescents with Divorced Parents." *School Counselor*, v35, n4, pp. 246–252, Mar 1988.

Model of group counseling that can be easily implemented and is likely to be supported by parents, teachers, and administration.

Goldstein, Spraflein, Gershaw, and Klein. *Skill-Streaming the Adolescent.* Research Press, Champaign, Illinois, 1982.

This book presents a structured learning model involving a group skill-training approach for dealing with feelings, aggression, and stress. The four components of this model are: modeling, roleplay, performance feedback, and transfer of training. Detailed outlines of the group sessions and many concrete examples make this book a valuable resource. This approach to groups follows a psychoeducational model.

Gwynn, Carol, and Helen Brantley. "Effect of a Divorce Group Intervention for Elementary School Children." *Psychology in the Schools*, v24, n2, pp. 161–164, Apr 1987.

Children 9–11 who participated in this prevention educational support group showed significant decreases in depression, anxiety, and negative feelings about divorce as compared to control group.

Huey, Wayne. "Counseling Teenage Fathers: The Maximizing Life Experience (MALE) Group." *School Counselor*, v35, n1, pp. 40–47, Sept 1987.

Describes a group-counseling program for unwed teenage fathers. Understanding the emotional and legal aspects and becoming aware of available resources are the main topics. Decision making, problem solving, and reproduction are covered.

LeCroy, Craig. "Teaching Children Social Skills: A Game Format." *Social Work*, v32, n5, pp. 440–442, Sept 1987.

A game approach to group counseling that emphasizes social-skill training that is fun, exciting, and interesting. How to organize such games, beginning sessions, using board games, and evaluation are discussed.

Morse, Linda. "Working with Young Procrastinators: Elementary School Students Who Do Not Complete School Assignments." *Elementary School Guidance and Counseling*, v21, n3, pp. 221–228, Feb 1987.

Multi-modal group counseling used with students in grades 3–6. Students made progress in goal setting, attitude and behavior, and report card grades.

Ohlsen, Horne, and Lawe. *Group Counseling*. Holt, Rinehart, & Winston, New York, New York, 1988.

The group-counseling textbook is very thorough in its coverage of school counseling. Three chapters are particularly helpful to school counselors: structured groups, group counseling with children, and group counseling with adolescents.

Omizo, Michael and Sharon Omizo. "Group Counseling Effects on Self-concept and Social Behaviors Among Children with Learning Disabilities." *Journal of Humanistic Education and Development*, v26, n3, pp. 109–117, Mar 1988.

Group counseling focusing on self-concept and social behavior with 4th, 5th, and 6th graders with learning disabilities. Ten weekly group sessions resulted in significantly higher post-test scores on self-concept and interpersonal and task-related behavior than control group.

Omizo, Michael M. and others. "Teaching Children to Cope with Anger." *Elementary School Guidance and Counseling*, v22, n3, pp. 241–246, Feb 1988.

Group counseling focusing on cognitive behavior techniques, positive reinforcement, role playing, and modeling was effective in reducing aggressive and hostile behaviors in intermediate-grade children.

Prout, H., and Richard DeMartino. "A Meta-Analysis of School-based Studies of Psychotherapy." *Journal of School Psychology*, v24, n3, pp. 285–292, Fall 1986.

Meta-analysis of school-based studies of psychotherapy. Group and behavioral theory interventions that target observed behaviors and problem-solving abilities were more effective.

Reynolds, William, and Kevin Stark. "School-based Intervention Strategies for the Treatment of Depression in Children and Adolescents: School-based Affective and Social Interventions." *Special Services in the Schools*, v3, n3–4, pp. 69–88, Spr–Sum 1987.

An overview of studies that demonstrate the effectiveness of counseling interventions for young people with depression. Specific techniques described are: cognitive restructuring, relaxation training, self-evaluation training, self-monitoring, activity scheduling, and self-reinforcement training. Results of several group studies using these techniques are presented.

Rose, Steven. "Social Skill Training in Middle Childhood: A Structured Group Approach." *Journal for Specialists in Group Work*, v12, n4, pp. 144–149, Nov 1987.

Ten group sessions focus on assertiveness, conversing with adults, empathy, popularity, and acceptance among peers. Techniques include rehearsal, instruction, modeling, feedback, social rewards, coaching, assignments, and group contingencies.

Strother, Joanna, and Riley Harvill. "Support Groups for Relocated Adolescent Students: A Model for School Counselors." *Journal for Specialists in Group Work*, v11, n2, pp. 114–120, May 1986.

The format for a support group to assist relocated students in assimilating into their new school is presented.

Wilgus, Edward, and Vicki Shelley. "The Role of the Elementary School Counselor: Teacher Perceptions, Expectations, and Actual Functions." *School Counselor*, v35, n4, pp. 259–266, Mar 1988.

Teacher ranked individual and group counseling as top two actual and ideal counselor functions.

Williams, George Taylor, and others. "School Counselors Using Group Counseling with Family-School Problems." *School Counselor*, v35, n3, pp. 169–178, Jan 1988.

A family problem-solving and communication model for school counselors. The three components are: 1) stopping the disruption and learning appropriate behavior, 2) improving communication, and 3) moral development. Examples are provided for elementary, middle, and high school groups.

Bibliography

Cartledge, Gwendolyn, and JoAnne F. Milburn. "The Case for Social Skills in the Classroom: A Review." *Review of Educational Research*, Vol. 1, No. 1, Winter 1978, pp. 133–156.

Combs, A.W., and others. *Florida Studies in the Helping Professions* (University of Florida Monographs, Social Science, No. 37.) University of Florida Press, Gainesville, Florida, 1969.

Corey, Gerald. *Theory and Practice of Group Counseling.* Brooks/Cole Publishing Company, Belmont, California, 1985.

Corey, G., and others. *Group Techniques.* Brooks/Cole Publishing Company, Belmont, California, 1982.

Dinkmeyer, Don, and Edson Caldwell. *Developmental Counseling and Guidance: A Comprehensive School Approach.* McGraw-Hill, Inc., New York, New York, 1970.

Havighurst, Robert. *Human Development and Education.* Green and Company, New York, New York, 1953.

Hops, Hyman, and Joseph Cobb. "Initial Investigations into Academic Survival-Skill Training, Direct Instruction, and First-Grade Achievement." *Journal of Educational Psychology,* vol. 66, no. 4, 1974, pp. 548–553.

Kalb, Jonah, and David Viscott, M.D. *What Every Kid Should Know.* Houghton Mifflin Company, Boston, Massachusetts, 1976.

Luft, Joseph. *Group Processes: An Introduction to Group Dynamics.* Mayfield Publishing Company, San Francisco, California, 1984.

Maslow, A. *Toward a Psychology of Being.* Van Nostrand, New York, 1968.

Miller, Gary M., and Joseph C. Rotter. *The Middle School Counselor.* The Carroll Press, Cranston, Rhode Island, 1985.

Myrick, Robert D. *Developmental Guidance and Counseling: A Practical Approach.* Educational Media, Minneapolis, Minnesota, 1987.

Pietrofesa, John J., and others. *Guidance: An Introduction.* Chapter on Group Counseling. Houghton Mifflin Company, Boston, Massachusetts, 1980.

Prout, H., and Richard DeMartino. "A Meta-analysis of School-based Studies of Psychotherapy." *Journal of School Psychology,* vol. 24, no. 3, pp. 285–292, Fall 1986.

Purkey, William W., and John M. Novak. *Inviting School Success: A Self-Concept Approach to Teaching and Learning.* Wadsworth, Inc., Belmont, California, 1984.

Rogers, C., and others. *The Therapeutic Relationship and Its Impact.* University of Wisconsin Press, Madison, Wisconsin, 1967.

Shutz, W.C. *FIRO: A Three Dimensional Theory of Interpersonal Behavior,* 1958.

Thornburg, H. editor. *Preadolescent Development.* University of Arizona Press, Tucson, Arizona.

Trotzer, J.P. *The Counselor and the Group: Integrating Theory, Training and Practice.* Brooks/Cole Publishing, Monterey, California, 1977.

Truax, C.B., and R.R. Carkhuff. *Toward Effective Counseling and Psychotherapy: Training and Practice.* Adline, Chicago, Illinois, 1967.

Wooster, Arthur, and Anita Carson. "Improving Reading and Self-concept through Communication and Social Skill Training." *British Journal of Guidance and Counseling,* vol. 10, no. 1, Jan. 1982.

Yalom, Irvin D. *The Theory and Practice of Group Psychotherapy,* 2nd edition. Basic Books, Inc., New York, New York, 1975.